Illustrator:
Kelly McMahon

Editor:
Barbara M. Wally

Editorial Project Manager:
Ina Massler Levin, M.A.

Editor-in-Chief:
Sharon Coan, M.S. Ed.

Art Director:
Elayne Roberts

Cover Artist:
Larry Bauer

Product Manager:
Phil Garcia

Imaging:
Pete Sadony

Publishers:
Rachelle Cracchiolo, M.S. Ed.
Mary Dupuy Smith, M.S. Ed.

Alphabet Soup

A Teacher Resource Book

Preschool – Grade 2

Author:

Karen Turner

Teacher Created Materials, Inc.
P.O. Box 1040
Huntington Beach, CA   92647
ISBN-1-55734-189-3

©1996 Teacher Created Materials, Inc.   Made in U.S.A.

Teacher Created Materials

Table of Contents

Table of Contents *(cont.)*

Introduction

Alphabet Soup is an invaluable creative resource for teaching the letters and sounds of the alphabet. Its pages are filled with a variety of lesson ideas and reproducible pages designed for use with primary children. Each letter is introduced by a high-quality children's literature selection which features the letter to be studied in its title. Sounds are emphasized through multi-sensory activities that cross the curriculum, featuring specific activities in oral and written language, art, number concepts, and movement. Patterns for bulletin boards and learning activities are time savers for busy teachers.

This early childhood unit includes:

- **literature selections** — questions and activities for each story which increase comprehension and set the stage for exploring the letter sound
- **bulletin board ideas** — plans and patterns for student-created bulletin boards
- **group projects** — to foster cooperative learning
- **picture and sound cards** — reproducible for each sound to be studied
- **learning centers** — suggestions for activities that cross the curriculum

To keep this valuable resource intact so that it can be used year after year, you may wish to punch holes in the pages and store them in a three-ring binder.

Alphabet Activities A a – Z z

What Do You Hear?

This activity uses pictures and words to introduce the sound each letter makes. All of the children participate in holding up picture cards and saying a chant to become acquainted with the sound that they are studying. For letters with more than one sound (a, e, i, o, u, c, g), activities are given for each sound. The teacher may present them together, use them as separate lessons, or elect to use only one sound to meet specific classroom needs and objectives.

The Alphabet Has Astonishing Letters

The children follow specific directions to decorate construction paper or poster board with objects that begin with the sound that they are studying. Display their work on the wall or bulletin board.

Bulletin Boards

Make colorful, educational bulletin boards with the help of your class. The children will help you fill the bulletin board with pictures and art projects that begin with the letter sound that your class is studying.

Sounds and Pictures

Your students will be introduced to a friend, a person or animal, with each new letter sound that they learn. The children help their new friend find pictures from the picture board that begin with the same sound as their new friend and hang the pictures on a big object that starts with the designated letter sound. Challenge the children by adding pictures that begin with other letter sounds. If a picture does not begin with the designated sound, they feed the picture to the sound muncher.

Picture Board: Paint a 3 x 4 foot (92 cm x 1.22 m) piece of plywood. Screw cup hooks to the board in evenly spaced rows to hold the picture cards.

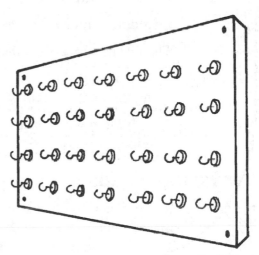

Sound Muncher: Use a box or container with an opening, like a trash can with a swinging door. Let the children help you decorate the sound muncher with eyes, hair, etc. Hot glue colorful large capital and lowercase letters to the outside of the sound muncher.

Alphabet Activities A a – Z z (cont.)

Sounds and Objects

Introduce your students to a variety of objects that start with the sound that they are studying. Add other objects that begin with different sounds and let the children decide whether the object begins with the letter sound that they are studying or another letter sound. Items beginning with the designated letter sound will be placed on an object that begins with the same sound. All other items will be fed to the sound muncher.

Letter Centers

A variety of creative experiences allow children to get to know each letter through art and play.

Let's Learn

The teacher asks the children questions or gives them directions to move or do a specific task. Before the children respond to each question or direction, ask them to identify which word or words begin with the sound being studied. Write these words on a wall chart or on the chalkboard.

Let's Talk	Encourage children to repeat the identified word when they respond.
Let's Move	The teacher directs children to move or act in a specific manner.
Let's Pretend	Children's imaginations soar when they are asked to pretend that they are using or doing things that begin with the letter that they are learning about.
Let's Do	The children will sort and group objects, correspond objects with numbers, and other activities.

Letter Picture Cards

Picture cards to be reproduced, colored, and laminated are provided for each sound. These are used in the What Do You Hear? and Sounds and Pictures activities. The cards can also be reproduced and used for the Bulletin Board section, if needed. A word list and blank master are also provided so that you can make additional cards for any letter. Challenge the children to find more words for each sound.

Patterns

Copy, color, and laminate patterns as needed for bulletin boards and the Sounds and Pictures activity.

Introducing the Letter A a

Letter A Literature: *There's Something in My Attic* by Mercer Mayer

Materials: one copy of the attic pattern for each child, crayons

Before reading *There's Something In My Attic*, discuss and make a list of items that are stored in attics: old toys, furniture, Christmas decorations, etc. Have the children draw pictures of items that are actually in an attic on one side of their papers. Discuss the things that can make an attic seem scary: dark, dirty, strange noises, etc. Make a list of things that they might imagine are in their attics, like monsters, witches, goblins, etc. Have the children turn their papers over and draw pictures of what they sometimes imagine is in their attics.

What Do You Hear?

(Short and long sounds may be presented separately.)

Materials: letter **A** long and short picture cards (reproduced, colored, and laminated)

Working with one set of cards at a time, show the children each picture card and ask them to name the object. Talk about the two sounds that the letter A makes. When sounding out the long **A**, tell the children that it says its own name, just like when they say the alphabet: A,B,C. When sounding out the short A sound, tell them it is the beginning of the sound that they make when they sneeze: achoo. Have the children practice the long and short **A** sounds.

Give each A card to a child. Pick one child to come up in front of the class. That child will show the rest of the class the picture card he/she is holding. The class responds with the chant "What Do You Hear?"

Short A

Class: "Astronaut, astronaut, what do you hear?"

(The student in front of the class looks at the remaining pictures and calls on one.)

Child: "I hear ant beginning like me."

Class: "Ant, ant, what do you hear?"

Child: "I hear apple beginning like me."

Continue until all of the short **A** picture cards have been called. The last child responds:

"I hear the letter **A** beginning with me."

The class adds: "We all hear the short **A** sound going a-a-a-a!"

What Do You Hear? *(cont.)*
Long A

Class: "Angel, angel, what do you hear?"

Child: "I hear ape beginning like me."

Class: "Ape, ape, what do you hear?"

Child: "I hear acorn beginning like me."

Continue until all of the long **A** pictures cards have been called. The last child responds:

"I hear the letter **A** beginning with me."

The class adds: "We all hear the long **A** sound going a-a-a-a!"

A Is an Astonishing Letter

Materials: large pieces of construction paper or poster board with a large capital and lowercase **A** printed on each; glue; **A** items (paper airplanes, arrows made of pipe cleaners, advertisements, acorns, angels, raisins for ants)

Divide the class into groups of four or five. The children work together to glue the **A** items on the **A a**. When the glue dries, display the pictures on a bulletin board or a wall.

Bulletin Board

Materials: crayons, markers, paper, scissors, glue, magazines, copies of picture cards or other short and long A worksheets, green and brown construction paper, copies of the acorn and apple patterns for each child

Use green and brown paper to make two large trees, and staple them to the bulletin board.

Make one large acorn. Write the following directions on the large acorn: *Please help decorate an acorn with pictures that begin with the long A sound.* Staple the acorn to the bottom of one tree trunk.

Make one large apple, and write the following directions on it: *Please help decorate an apple with pictures that begin with the short A sound.* Staple the apple to the bottom of the other tree trunk.

Introducing the Letter A a *(cont.)*

Bulletin Board *(cont.)*

Show the bulletin board to the children and explain the directions to them.

Have the children cut out their apples and acorns. Ask the children to decorate their apples and acorns with pictures that begin with the letter **A**, using pictures that they have drawn, pictures cut from magazines or worksheets that they have colored. Staple their finished apples and acorns on the bulletin board.

The children can search at home for additional pictures that begin with **A** to add to the bulletin board.

Sounds and Pictures

(For older or more advanced students, short and long sounds may be presented together)

Materials: Reproduced, colored, and laminated ape, ant, and ambulance patterns; cloth apron or laminated apron pattern; short and long **A** picture cards; several non-**A** picture cards; Velcro; hole punch; picture board; sound muncher

Punch a hole at the top of each long and short **A** picture card and hot glue a piece of Velcro to the back. Glue the matching Velcro piece to the apron or the ambulance.

Mix the long and short **A** picture cards and hang them on the picture board.

Hang the apron and the ambulance on the wall where the children can see and touch them.

Place the ant by the ambulance and the ape by the apron.

Gather the children by the ape, apron, ant, ambulance, and the picture board.

Short A

Tell the children: "I would like you to meet Astonishing Ant.
He is an astonishing ant because he can drive an ambulance. He drives his ambulance every afternoon through apple orchards, and around aquariums and adults. As Astonishing drives, he makes a special ă–ă–ă–ă sound. (Have the children pretend to drive and make the short sound like Astonishing does.) Astonishing has brought his ambulance with him today because he wants us to help him decorate it with pictures that begin with the short A sound. Can you help Astonishing Ant decorate his ambulance with pictures that start with the same sound as ant, ambulance, and the sound he makes when he is driving his ambulance, ă–ă–ă–ă?"

Introducing the Letter A a *(cont.)*

Sounds and Pictures *(cont.)*

As you point to each picture on the board, the children name the object. Repeat the word emphasizing the beginning sound of each picture card. Call the children one at a time to come up to the picture board and pick out a card. If it begins with a short **A**, have them stick it on the ambulance while Astonishing Ant and the children make the special ă–ă–ă–ă sound.

Long A

Tell the children: "Another visitor today is A+ Ape.

A+ Ape can cook almost any type of food and make it taste delicious. Everyone calls him A+ because he is an excellent cook. Before A+ Ape cooks anything, he always puts on his apron. You can hear him make a special sound ā–ā–ā–ā as he puts on his apron each morning. (Have the children pretend to put on an apron while they make the long sound like A+ does.) A+ has brought his apron with him today because he needs our help. He wants us to help him decorate his apron with pictures that begin with the long **A** sound. Can you help A+ decorate his apron with pictures that start with the same sound as ape, apron, and the special sound he makes, ā–ā–ā–ā?"

As you point to each picture on the board, the children name the object. Repeat the word emphasizing the beginning sound of each picture card. Call the children one at a time to come up to the picture board and pick out a card.

If it begins with a long **A**, have them stick it on the apron while A+ Ape while the children make the special a–a–a–a sound.

Leave A+ Ape, Astonishing Ant, the apron and the ambulance out in the classroom.

After you have done this activity several times, mix up the pictures on the apron and ambulance.

Tell the children: "Astonishing Ant went racing in his ambulance and drove so fast that all the pictures blew off of his ambulance and A+'s apron. The pictures got all mixed up, so they tried to stick them back up in the proper places, but they are not sure if they did it correctly."

Ask the children to look at the apron and the ambulance and identify any pictures which need to be moved from the long **A** apron to the short **A** ambulance or vice versa.

Introducing the Letter A a *(cont.)*

Sounds and Pictures *(cont.)*

If you want to challenge your class even more, add some non-A picture cards to both the apron and the ambulance. Tell the students that the A pictures were mixed up with other picture cards. When they find a non-A picture card on the ambulance or apron, have them feed it to the sound muncher. The children make the beginning sound of the non-A picture as the sound muncher eats it.

Sounds and Objects

Long A

Materials: a large, laminated desktop paper calendar for the month of April; objects that begin with the long A sound (ace, acorn, angel, angel food cake, ape, apron, toy or paper airplane)

Short A

Materials: a large arrow made of laminated poster board; objects that begin with the short A sound (anchor, ant, asparagus, plastic ax, avocado, toy alligator, apples, applesauce)

Place all of the A objects on the April calendar and the arrow. Have the children name each object as you show it to the class. Repeat the word emphasizing the long or short sound at the beginning. As the objects are named, place them on a table.

Each child comes up to the table, selects an object and says its name. If it begins like April, have them place it on the calendar page. If it begins like arrow, have them place it on the arrow.

When you feel that the children can distinguish between the long and short A sounds, you may decide to challenge them by adding several objects that begin with other sounds. If a child picks up one of these objects, he/she can feed it to the sound muncher. The child or the class makes the beginning sound of the non-A object as it is being eaten.

Leave the calendar page, arrow, and all of the A objects out as a display in the classroom.

Introducing the Letter A a (cont.)

Letter Centers

Apple Prints

Materials: cut apples; red, yellow, and green paint; paper

Children dip apple slices into the paint and press on paper.

Apple Cereal Necklace

Materials: apple-flavored cereal, string or yarn

Children string yarn through the holes in the cereal. Let them eat their creations like a candy necklace.

Ant Tracks

Materials: raisins, brown paint, brown fine-line markers, paper

Children dip raisins into the brown paint and press on paper. After the paint dries they use markers to add legs and antennae on the ants.

A a Play Dough

Materials: play dough, acorns, cookie cutters in shapes that begin with the long and short letter **A** (apple, ax, astronaut, etc.)

Children press acorns and cookie cutters into the play dough to make pictures and patterns. They can also roll out the dough to form the capital and lowercase letters **A a**.

Let's Learn

Before they respond to each question or direction that you give them, ask the children to identify which word or words begin with an A. Write the A words on a wall chart or on the chalkboard.

Let's Talk

- Name something that makes you angry. (tattlers, brother or sister, fights, when people lie)

- Tell me something that you do after school. (play ball, read a book, take a gym or dance class)

- Name your favorite animal. (dog, cat, hampster, monkey, lion, kangaroo)

- Describe an alien from outer space.

- Who is your favorite television or movie actor?

Introducing the Letter A a *(cont.)*

Let's Learn *(cont.)*

Let's Talk *(cont.)*

- What are some things you are able to do by yourself? (tie shoes, brush teeth, get dressed)
- Name a place where an astronaut might go. (the moon, Mars, outer space)
- Tell me about an adventure you have had.
- What do you do when someone asks a question? (answer it)

Let's Move

- Move around the room like an alligator, ape, ant, and anteater.

Let's Pretend

Pretend to:
- shoot an arrow
- chop down an apple tree with an ax
- put on an apron
- fly an airplane

Let's Do

- Count apple cereal pieces out to correspond with oral or written numbers.
- Take a class apple survey. Have the children pick out their favorite way to eat apples: sliced up, as applesauce, baked. Record their responses on an "Apple Graph."

APPLE	Jan	Sue	Pete	Sal
SLICED	✔			
BAKED			✔	
APPLE SAUCE				
APPLE PIE		✔		
WHOLE APPLE				✔

- Make up a class tongue twister using long A words: *The angel gave aid to the aching ape.*
- Make up a class tongue twister using short A words: *anteater asks for ants, apples, and asparagus around the ambulance.*

Introducing the Letter A a (cont.)

Short A Picture Cards

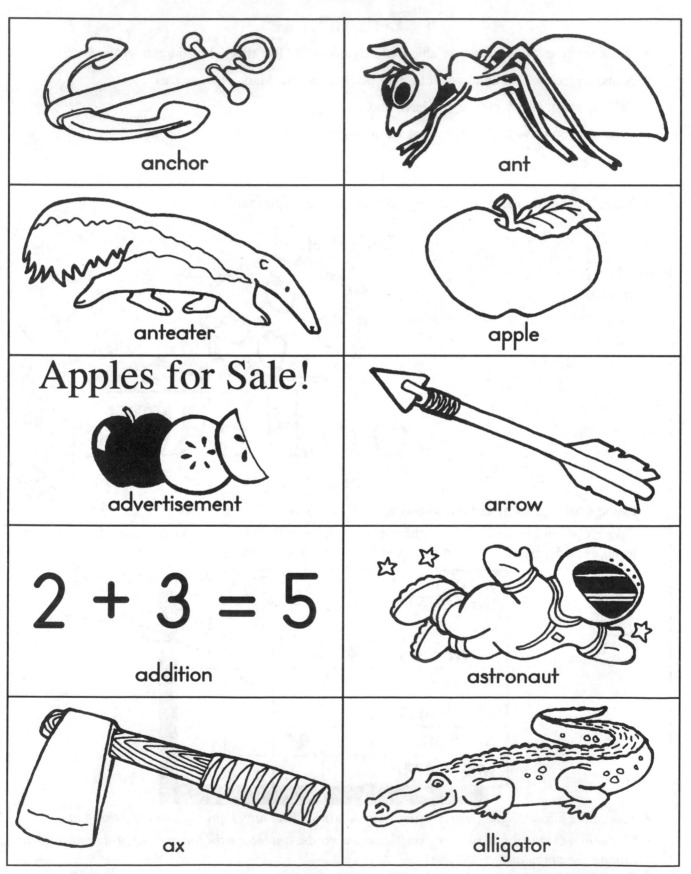

anchor

ant

anteater

apple

Apples for Sale!

advertisement

arrow

2 + 3 = 5

addition

astronaut

ax

alligator

Introducing the Letter A a *(cont.)*

Long A Picture Cards

ace

acorn

April

ache

ape

angel

apron

airplane

Introducing the Letter A a (cont.)

Patterns

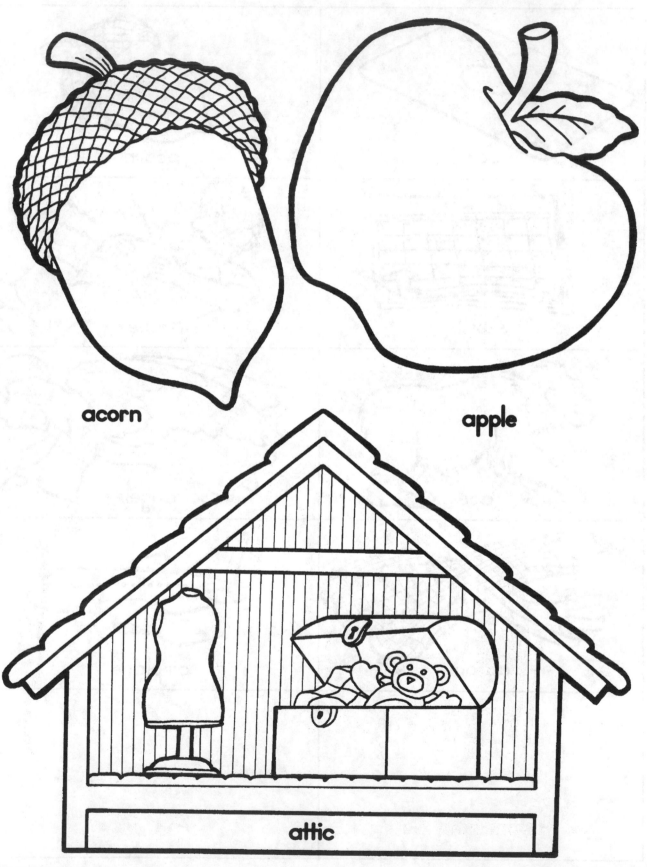

acorn

apple

attic

Introducing the Letter A a *(cont.)*

ambulance

apron pattern

Astonishing Ant

A+ Ape

Introducing the Letter B b

Letter B Literature: *The Bear's Bike* by Emilie Warren McLeod

Before reading *The Bear's Bike*, show the book to the children and ask them to identify the two B pictures on the cover. Have the children predict what they think this book is going to be about. After reading the story, make a list of all the good bike safety tips that they learned from this story.

What Do You Hear?

Materials: letter **B** picture cards (reproduced, colored, and laminated)

Talk about the sound that the letter **B** makes. Show the children each picture card and ask them to name the object. Repeat the word, emphasizing the **B** sound.
Give each card to a child. Pick one child to come up in front of the class. That child shows the rest of the class the picture card he/she is holding. The class responds with the chant "What Do You Hear?"

Class: "Baby, baby, what do you hear?" (The child in front of the class looks at the remaining pictures and calls on one.)

Child: "I hear book beginning like me."

Class: "Book, book, what do you hear?"

Child: "I hear bottle beginning like me."

Continue until all of the picture cards have been called. The last child responds with: "I hear the letter B beginning with me." The class adds at the end: "We all hear the **B** sound going b–b–b–b!"

B Is a Beautiful Letter

Materials: large pieces of construction paper or poster board with a large capital and lowercase **B** printed on each, glue, **B** items (beans, balloons, beads, bandages, buttons, small jewelry boxes, brads, branches, small pieces of hardened bread, brown bags, bows, burlap)

Divide the class into groups of 4 or 5. The children work together to glue the **B** items on top of the **B b**. When the glue dries, display the pictures on a bulletin board or a wall.

Introducing the Letter B b *(cont.)*

Bulletin Board

Materials: crayons, markers, paper, scissors, magazines, copies of picture cards or other **B** worksheets, glue, a panel from a cardboard box, colorful stringed beads, one copy of the ball pattern for each child

Staple the cardboard box panel to the bulletin board. Make a border with the beads.

Make one large copy of the ball. Write the following directions on the ball: *Please help fill the big, brown box with bouncy beach balls decorated with beautiful pictures that begin with the letter B.*

Staple the ball to the center of the box. Show the bulletin board to the children and explain the directions to them.

Have the children cut out their balls and decorate them with pictures that begin with the letter **B**, using pictures that they have drawn, pictures cut from magazines, or worksheets that they have colored. Staple their finished balls on the bulletin board.

The children can search at home for additional pictures that begin with the letter **B** to be added to the bulletin board.

Sounds and Pictures

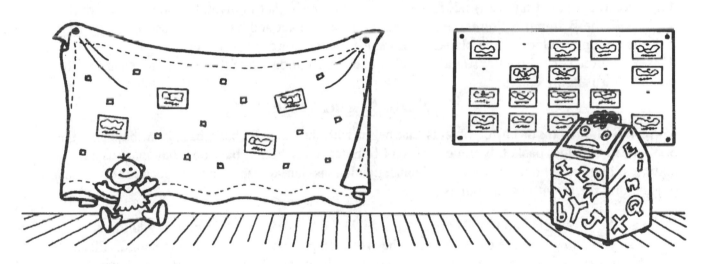

Materials: baby doll, blanket, **B** picture cards, some non–**B** picture cards, Velcro, hole punch, picture board, sound muncher

Punch a hole at the top of each picture card and hot glue a Velcro piece to the back of each. Hot glue the matching Velcro pieces to the blanket.

Place most of the **B** picture cards and some non–**B** picture cards on the picture board. Save a few **B** picture cards and several non–**B** picture cards to be added later.

Hang the baby blanket on the wall where the children can see and touch it. Place the baby doll beside the blanket.

Gather the children by the blanket, baby doll, picture board, and sound muncher.

Introducing the Letter B b *(cont.)*

Sounds and Pictures *(cont.)*

Tell the children: "I would like you to meet Bitsy Baby."

"Bitsy Baby is a special baby because when she is happy, she does not sound like other babies. Instead of saying goo–goo, she makes the sound b–b–b–b. (Have the children make the b–b–b–b sound like Bitsy.) She has brought her blanket with her today because she needs our help. She isn't happy because her baby blanket is empty. She wants her baby blanket to be filled with beautiful pictures that begin with the letter **B**. Can you help her decorate her blanket with pictures that start with the same sound as a baby, blanket, and the sound she makes when she is happy, b–b–b–b?"

As you point to each picture on the board, the children name the object. Repeat the word, emphasizing the beginning sound of each picture. Call the children one at a time to come up to the picture board and pick out a card. If it begins with a **B**, the child sticks it on the blanket while Bitsy Baby and the children make the special b–b–b–b sound. If it does not begin with a **B**, he/she feeds it to the sound muncher. The child or the class makes the appropriate beginning sound while the picture is being eaten.

Leave the blanket and baby out in the classroom. After you have done this activity several times, mix up the pictures on the blanket and add some more **B** pictures and several non–**B** pictures to the blanket.

Tell the children: "Bitsy Baby added some more pictures to her blanket, but she is not sure if they all begin with the **B** sound." Point to each picture on the blanket and have the class say the word with you. Ask the children to look at the blanket and identify any pictures which need to be removed and fed to the sound muncher. Have the sound muncher and the children make the beginning sound of the non-**B** picture as it is being eaten.

Sounds and Objects

Materials: large box or barrel, objects that begin with the letter **B** (bear, bag, bow, bandage, button, book, beads, badge, basket, barrette, bottle of bubbles, baby bottle, balloons, banana, basketball, batteries, bell, belt, boot, bowl, bone, beans, bandannas, burlap, backpack, barbecue sauce,), several objects that begin with other sounds

Place all the **B** objects and non–**B** objects inside the box. Have the children tell you the name for each object as you show it to the class. Repeat the word, emphasizing the beginning sound. Place all of the objects on a table after you have introduced them to the class. Turn the box upside down.

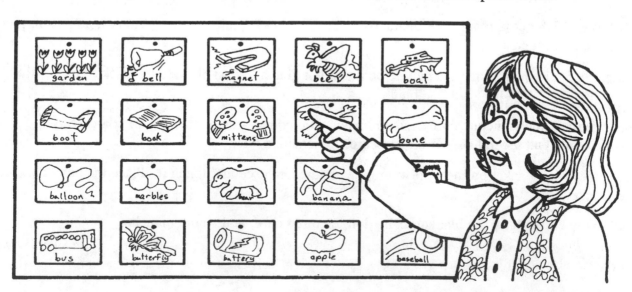

Introducing the Letter B b *(cont.)*

Sounds and Objects *(cont.)*

Each child comes up to the table, selects an object, and says its name. If it begins like box, the child places it on the box. If it does not begin like box, he/she feeds it to the sound muncher. Have the child or the class make the beginning sound of the non-B object as it is being eaten.

Leave the box and all of the **B** objects out as a display in the classroom.

Letter Centers

Burlap Block Prints

Materials: blue, brown, and black paint; blocks with burlap glued to the bottom, paper

Children dip burlap blocks into blue, black, and brown paints and press onto paper. They can form the letters **B b** and make pictures that start with the **B** sound.

B b Play Dough

Materials: brown, blue, and black play dough and/or biscuit dough, beans, blocks, buttons, beads, biscuit cutters, cookie cutters in shapes that begin with the letter **B** (butterfly, birthday cake, bear, etc.)

Children press **B** objects, biscuit cutters and cookie cutters into the play dough and/or biscuit dough to make patterns, pictures, and biscuits. They can also roll out the dough to form the capital and lowercase letters **B b**.

Bear

Materials: teddy bear; a bag containing a bonnet, bracelet, booties, beads, badge, button, bandanna, bow, barrette, and bandage

Children take the items out of the bag and dress and decorate the bear with **B** items.

Beans

Materials: paper with an outline of a bean drawn on it

Children trace the bean outline with glue, place the beans on top of the glue and let it dry.

Let's Learn

Before they respond to each question or direction that you give them, ask the children to identify which word or words begin with a **B**. Write the **B** words on a wall chart or on the chalkboard.

Introducing the Letter B b *(cont.)*

Let's Learn *(cont.)*

Let's Talk

- Have you ever been stung by a bumblebee? How did it feel?
- Name a body part that your clothes do not cover. (hands, nose, ears, face)
- Name something that you could see at the beach. (sand, umbrellas, water, shells)
- Name something that you could see in or around a barn. (haystack, cows, fence, chickens)
- Name something that needs a battery to work. (flashlights, car, toys)
- Name something that you would need to take a bath. (water, soap, shampoo, washcloth)
- Name a type of bread. (white, rye, wheat)
- Name a type of ball. (football, basketball, softball)
- Name something that you can bake. (cookies, cake, pie)
- Name something that you do before you go to bed. (brush your teeth, take bath, read book)
- Name your favorite bedtime book.

Let's Move

- Step, walk, hop, and jump backwards.
- Walk around the room like a baby bear, momma bear, and/or daddy bear.
- Lay down on the floor and sizzle like a piece of bacon that is getting hotter and hotter in a frying pan.
- Crawl on the floor like a baby
- Bounce up and down, fast then slow
- Walk around the room like you are on a balance beam.
- Fly around the room like a butterfly.

Let's Pretend

Pretend to:

- bounce a ball
- button and unbutton your shirt
- build a building with blocks
- stick a wand into a bottle of bubbles and blow them all over

- put on a bandage
- blow up a balloon
- eat a biscuit (don't forget the butter)
- brush your teeth, hair

Let's Do

- Play bingo.
- Make a class banner: "We Are Sound Experts." Have each child sign his/her name and hang it in the classroom.
- Group buttons according to size, color, number of holes, shape, and texture.
- Count out beans, buttons, or blocks to correspond with oral or written numbers.
- Sing "Happy Birthday." Call out each month, and have the children stand when they hear their birthday months. Make a "Birthday Graph."
- Make up a class tongue twister using **B** words: Brave baby bumblebee buzzed by the barn, beach, and baseball field.

Introducing the Letter B b (cont.)

Letter B Picture Cards

baby

ballerina

bear

bee

bird

balloon

butterfly

baseball

button

battery

Introducing the Letter B b *(cont.)*

Letter B Picture Cards *(cont.)*

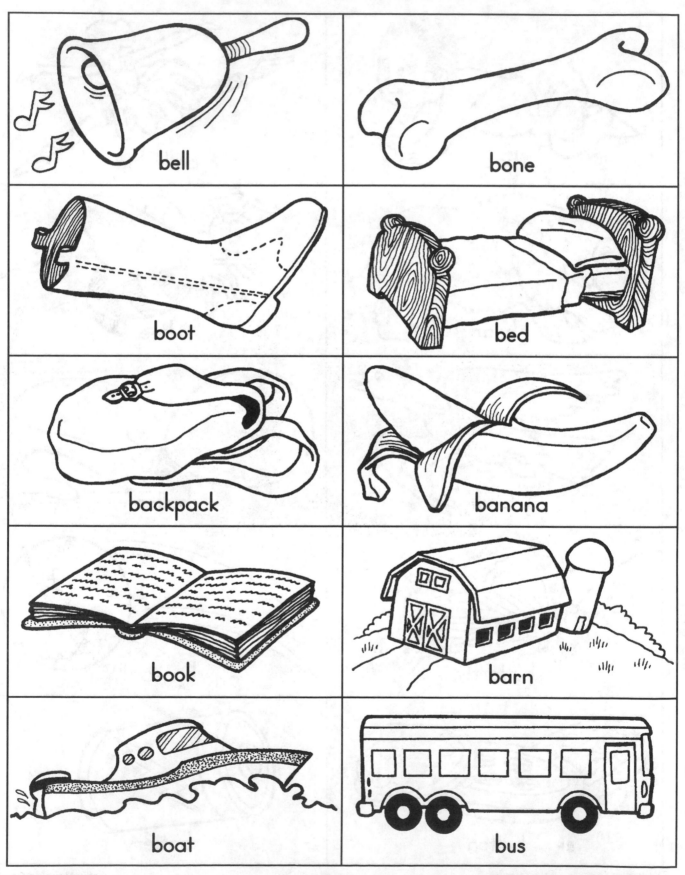

bell

bone

boot

bed

backpack

banana

book

barn

boat

bus

Introducing the Letter B b *(cont.)*

Patterns

ball

Introducing the Letter C c

Letter C Literature: *The Very Hungry Caterpillar* by Eric Carle

Materials: one copy of the caterpillar for each child, magazines or newspapers with food pictures

Look at the cover of the book. Read the title and ask the children to find a word that begins with a **C** sound. After reading the story, talk about the stages (egg, caterpillar, cocoon, butterfly) the caterpillar went through before it became a butterfly. See if the children can remember any of the food items that the caterpillar ate. Sort the food into groups such as fruit, meat, sweets, and dairy. Name foods that start with a **C** sound: cake, cone, and cupcake.

Give each child a caterpillar. Ask them to find pictures of foods that begin with the soft **C** sound (celery, cereal, cinnamon, cider) and/or the hard **C** sound (crackers, corn, cone, coffee, cauliflower, cantaloupe, candy, cabbage, cake) and glue them to the caterpillar.

What Do You Hear?

(Hard and soft sounds may be presented separately.)

Materials: soft and hard sound letter **C** picture cards (reproduced, colored, and laminated)

Working with one set of cards at a time, show the children each picture card and ask them to name the object. Repeat the word emphasizing the **C** sound. Talk about the two different sounds that the letter **C** makes.

Give each card to a child. Pick one child to come up in front of the class. That child will show the rest of the class the picture he/she is holding. The class responds with the chant "What Do You Hear?"

Hard C

Class: "Carrot, carrot, what do you hear?" (The child in the front of the class looks at the remaining pictures and calls on one.)

Child: "I hear cactus beginning like me."

Class: "Cactus, cactus, what do you hear?"

Child: "I hear cotton beginning like me."

Continue until all of the hard **C** picture cards have been called. The last child responds: "I hear the letter **C** beginning with me." The class adds: "We all hear the hard **C** going c–c–c–c!"

Introducing the Letter C c *(cont.)*

What Do You Hear? *(cont.)*

Soft C

Class: "Circle, circle, what do you hear?"

Child: "I hear cereal beginning like me."

Class: "Cereal, cereal, what do you hear?"

Child: "I hear cymbal beginning like me."

Continue until all of the soft C picture cards have been called. The last child responds: "I hear the letter C beginning with me."

The class adds: "We all hear the soft C sound going c–c–c–c!"

C Is a Cute Letter!

Materials: large pieces of construction paper or poster board with a large capital and lowercase C printed on each, glue, C items (cotton, corn kernels, coupons, greeting cards, candles, playing cards, caps from bottles, candy wrappers, small pieces of carpet, cereal, clothespins, confetti, cornflakes, crackers, cellophane, etc.)

Divide the class into groups of four or five. The children work together to glue the C items on the C c. When the glue dries, display the pictures on a bulletin board or a wall.

Bulletin Board

Materials: crayons, markers, scissors, magazines, copies of picture cards or other hard and soft C worksheets, glue, copies of the camera and certificate patterns for each child

Make one large copy of the camera, and write the following directions on the lens: *Please help decorate a cool camera with pictures that begin with the hard C sound.*

Make one large copy of the certificate and write the following directions on it: *Please decorate a certificate with pictures that begin with the soft C sound.*

Staple the large camera and certificate to the bulletin board. Show the bulletin board to the children and explain the directions to them.

Have the children cut out their cameras and certificates and decorate the cameras with hard C pictures and the certificates with soft C pictures. They can use pictures that they have drawn, pictures cut from magazines, or worksheets that they have colored. Staple their finished cameras and certificates on the bulletin board.

The children can search at home for additional C pictures to be added to the bulletin board.

Introducing the Letter C c *(cont.)*

Sounds and Pictures

(For older or more advanced students, hard and soft sounds may be presented together.)

Materials: stuffed cat, curtains or material to resemble curtains, Cindy (reproduced, colored, and laminated Cindy pattern), several empty cereal boxes, hard and soft **C** picture cards, Velcro, hole punch, picture board, sound muncher

Punch a hole near the top of each card and hot glue a piece of Velcro to the back. Hot glue the matching Velcro pieces to the curtains or the cereal boxes.

Hang the curtains and the boxes of cereal on the wall where the children can see and touch them. Place the stuffed cat beside the curtains and Cindy by the cereal boxes.

Gather the children by the curtains, cat, Cindy, cereal, picture board, and sound muncher.

Hard C

Tell the children: "I would like you to meet Cuddly Cat. Cuddly Cat is a special cat because instead of purring when she is content, she makes a special c–c–c–c sound. (Have the children make the hard sound like Cuddly does.) Cuddly loves to claw and climb on her curtains. She has come here today to ask us for help. She heard that we are very smart when it comes to letters and sounds. She wants us to decorate her curtains with pictures that begin with the hard **C** sound. Can you help Cuddly decorate her curtains with pictures that start with the same sound as cat, curtains and the sound she makes when she is content, c–c–c–c?"

As you point to each picture on the board, the children name the object. Repeat the word, emphasizing the beginning hard or soft **C** sound of each picture. Call the children one at a time to come up to the picture board and pick out a card. If the picture begins with a hard **C**, the child sticks it on the curtains while Cuddly Cat and the children make the hard **C** sound.

Soft C

Tell the children: "Cereal Cindy is another visitor. Cereal Cindy is a little girl who loves to eat cereal. You can hear Cindy make a c–c–c–c sound when she eats her cereal. (Have the children pretend to eat spoonfuls of cereal and make the soft sound like Cindy does.) Cindy has brought in her cereal boxes today because she wants us to decorate them with pictures that begin with the soft **C** sound. Can you help Cindy decorate her cereal boxes with pictures that start with the same sound as Cindy, cereal, and the sound she makes when she eats her cereal, c–c–c–c?"

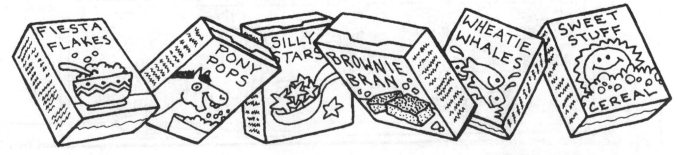

Introducing the Letter C c *(cont.)*

Sounds and Pictures *(cont.)*

As you point to each picture on the board, the children name the object. Repeat the word, emphasizing the beginning hard or soft C sound of each picture. Call the children one at a time to come up to the picture board and pick out a card. If the picture begins with a soft C, he/she sticks it on a cereal box. Cereal Cindy and the children make the soft C sound when a soft C picture is added to her cereal boxes.

Leave the cat, curtains, Cindy, and the cereal boxes out in the classroom.

After you have done this activity several times, mix up the hard and soft C picture cards and stick them back on the curtains and cereal boxes.

Tell the children: "When Cuddly Cat climbed up her curtains and looked in the cereal boxes, she accidentally knocked down all of the picture cards. She tried to return them to the right places, but she is not sure if she did it correctly."

Ask the children to look at the curtains and the cereal boxes and identify any pictures which need to be moved from the hard C curtains to the soft C cereal boxes or vice versa.

If you want to challenge your class even more, add some non–C picture cards to the curtains and the cereal boxes. Tell the children that the C pictures were mixed up with other picture cards. When the children find a non–C picture card on the curtains or cereal boxes, have them feed it to the sound muncher. The child or the class makes the beginning sound of the non–C picture as it is being eaten.

Sounds and Objects

Hard C

Materials: carpet piece, objects that begin with hard C (carrot, camera, cactus, candy, cup, comb, coupons, card, coat, cap, corn, can, calendar, candle, cane, canteen, car, catalog, etc.)

Soft C

Materials: circle cut from poster board, objects that begin with soft C (cinnamon, cereal, cylinder, cider, celery, certificate, cedar, cellophane, cement mix, cent, ceramics, cymbals)

Place the circle and the carpet piece on the floor. Place all of the objects in random order on the circle and carpet. Show each object to the class. Have the children tell you the name of each object as you show it to the class. As each object is introduced, place it on a table.

Introducing the Letter C c *(cont.)*

Sounds and Objects *(cont.)*

Each child comes up to the table, selects an object, and says its name. If it begins like carpet, the child places it on the carpet. If it begins like circle, he/she places it on the circle.

Anytime you feel that the children can distinguish between the hard and soft **C** sounds, you may decide to challenge them by adding into the group objects that begin with other sounds. If a child picks up one of these objects, he/she can feed it to the sound muncher. Have the child or class make the beginning sound of the non–**C** object as it is being eaten.

Leave the circle, carpet, and all of the **C** items out as a display in the classrooom.

Learning Centers

Coins And Coupons

Materials: coupons, play or real coins, crayons, paper

Children match up coins to the amount of savings on different coupons. Have the children make their own coupons on paper for various products.

Class Catalog

Materials: construction paper, crayons or markers

Each child designs a page for a class catalog, drawing a picture of an item and giving information about cost, colors, age group, etc. Assemble the pages into a book and design a cover for your class catalog.

C c Play Dough

Materials: play dough, corn kernels, coins, caps, cookie cutters in shapes that begin with the letter **C** (cat, cookie, coin, etc.)

Children press **C** objects in the play dough to make pictures and patterns. They can also roll out the dough to form letters **C c** in the dough.

Let's Learn

Before they respond to each question or direction that you give them, ask the children to identify which word or words begin with a **C**. Write the **C** words on a wall chart or on the chalkboard.

Introducing the Letter C c *(cont.)*

Let's Learn *(cont.)*

Let's Talk

- Name something that makes you cry. (onions, sad movie, pain)
- Name an animal that you might see in a cage at the zoo or pet shop. (monkey, lion, dog)
- Name some items that you would take on a camping trip. (sleeping bags, tent, flashlight)
- Name something that you take care of by yourself. (garden, dog, room)
- What is a compliment? What should you say after someone gives you a compliment? (thank you)
- Name something that can be cut. (paper, meat, hair)
- Name a kind of cookie. (chocolate chip, peanut butter, sugar)
- Name a kind of candy. (gum drops, jelly beans, chocolate bars, licorice)

Let's Move

- Crawl or creep across the floor.
- Move around the room like you are a cat or camel.
- Clap your hands fast, then slowly.

Let's Pretend

Pretend to:

- eat cotton candy
- mix, bake, and eat cookies
- catch a caterpillar (let it walk up your arm)
- put on your coat
- cut a piece of cake
- open up a can of carrots
- eat corn on the cob

Let's Do

- Play card games.
- Count out crayons, cotton balls, caps, or pieces of candy to correspond with oral or written numbers.
- Graph favorite colors. Have each child color in a section on a circle graph with his/her favorite color.
- Make up a class tongue twister using hard C words: Crabby Cat can cross-stitch calendars.
- Make up a class tongue twister using soft C words: The center of the circus was filled with cement cylinders.

Introducing the Letter C c *(cont.)*

Hard C Picture Cards

car

candle

cow

cat

cookie

camera

cactus

candy

camel

comb

Introducing the Letter C c *(cont.)*

Soft C Picture Cards

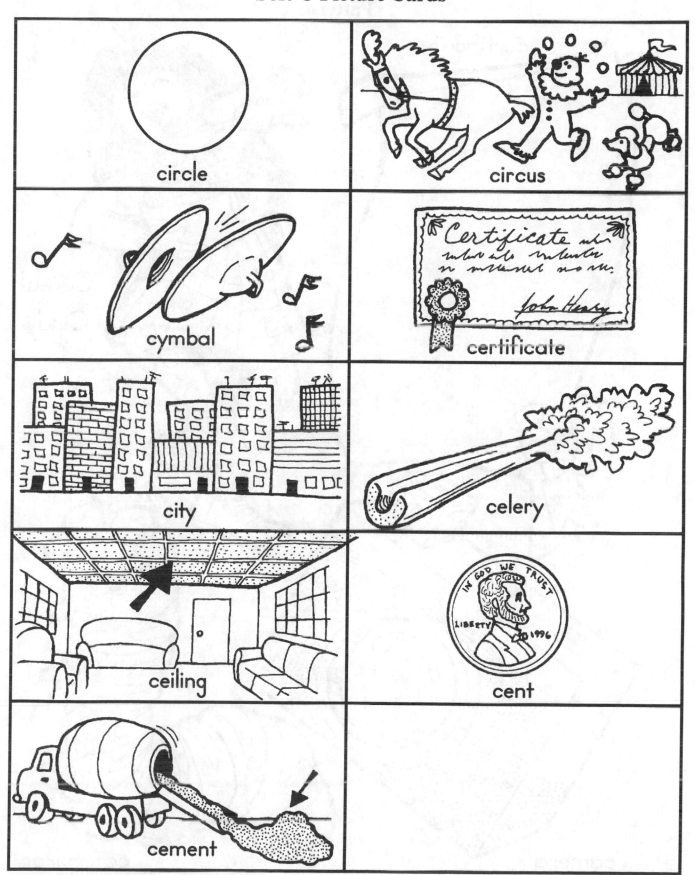

circle

circus

cymbal

certificate

city

celery

ceiling

cent

cement

Introducing the Letter C c *(cont.)*

Patterns

certificate

Cereal
Cindy

camera

caterpillar

34

Introducing the Letter D d

Letter D Literature: *Dreams* by Ezra Jack Keats

Materials: construction paper, crayons

After reading *Dreams*, let the children talk about dreams that they have had. Have the children express their good dreams by drawing them on paper.

What Do You Hear?

Materials: letter **D** picture cards (reproduced, colored, and laminated)

Talk about the sound that the letter **D** makes. Show the children each picture card and ask them to name the object. Repeat the word emphasizing the **D** sound.

Give each card to a child. Pick one child to come up in front of the class. That child will show the rest of the class the picture card he/she is holding. The class responds with the chant "What Do You Hear?"

Class: "Daffodil, daffodil, what do you hear?" (The child in the front of the class looks at the remaining pictures and calls on one.)

Child: "I hear doctor beginning like me."

Class: "Doctor, doctor, what do you hear?"

Child: "I hear diamond beginning like me."

Continue until all of the picture cards have been called. The last child responds: "I hear the letter **D** beginning with me."

The class adds: "We all hear the **D** sound going d–d–d–d!"

D Is a Distinguished Letter!

Materials: large pieces of construction paper or poster board with a large capital and lowercase **D** printed on each, glue, **D** items: dimes and dollars (play money or shapes cut from aluminum foil and green construction paper), diamond shapes, dice, dirt, paper donuts, down feathers, dots, pieces cut from a diaper

Divide the class into groups of four or five. The children work together to glue the **D** items on the **D d**. When the glue dries, display the pictures on a bulletin board or a wall.

Introducing the Letter D d *(cont.)*

Bulletin Board

Materials: crayons, markers, paper, scissors, magazines, copies of picture cards or other **D** worksheets, glue, one copy of the dollar pattern for each child

Make one large copy of the dollar. Write the following directions on the large dollar: *Please help decorate a dollar with pictures that begin with the letter* **D**.

Staple the large dollar in the center of the bulletin board. Show the bulletin board to the children and explain the directions to them.

Give each child a copy of the dollar. Ask the children to decorate their dollars with pictures that begin with the letter **D**, using pictures that they have drawn, pictures cut from magazines, or worksheets that they have colored. Staple their finished dollars to the bulletin board.

The children can search at home for additional pictures that begin with **D** to add to the bulletin board.

Sounds and Pictures

Materials: dog (use a stuffed one or reproduce, color, and laminate the dog pattern), dress (use a child's dress or cut and color the pattern), **D** picture cards, some non–**D** picture cards, Velcro, hole punch, picture board, sound muncher

Punch a hole near the top of each card and hot glue a Velcro piece to the back. Hot glue the matching Velcro pieces to the dress.

Place most of the **D** picture cards and some non–**D** picture cards on the picture board. Save a few **D** picture cards and several non–**D** picture cards to be added later.

Hang the dress on the wall where the children can see and touch it. Place the dog by the dress. Gather the children by the dress, dog, picture board, and sound muncher.

Tell the children: "I would like you to meet Designer Dog. Designer Dog is different from other dogs because she likes to design dresses instead of digging in the dirt. When she designs dresses she barks like this: d–d–d–d. (Have the children pretend to design a dress and make the d–d–d–d sound like Designer Dog does.) She has brought a dress with her today because she needs our help. She isn't happy with this dress because it is too dull looking. She wants to decorate the dress with pictures that begin with the letter **D** so it will look distinguished. Can you help her decorate the dress with pictures that start with the same sound as dog, dress, and the sound she makes when she barks, d–d–d–d?"

Introducing the Letter D d (cont.)

Sounds and Pictures (cont.)

As you point to each picture on the board, the children name the object. Repeat the word, emphasizing the beginning sound of each picture card. Call the children one at a time to come up to the picture board and pick out a card. If it begins with a **D**, have them stick it on the dress while Designer Dog and the children make the special d–d–d–d sound. If it does not begin with a **D**, have them feed it to the sound muncher. The child or the class makes the appropriate beginning sound while the picture is being eaten.

Leave the dress and Designer Dog out in the classroom. After you have done this activity several times, mix up the pictures on the dress and add some more **D** pictures and several non–**D** pictures to the dress.

Tell the children: "Designer Dog added some more pictures to her dress, but she is not sure if they all begin with the **D** sound."

Point to each picture on the dress and have the class say the word with you. Ask the children to look at the dress and identify any pictures which need to be removed and fed to the sound muncher. Have the sound muncher and the children make the beginning sound of the non–**D** picture as it is being eaten.

Sounds and Objects

Materials: desk, objects that begin with the letter **D** (dishes, dinosaur, dime, dollar, duck, doll, diaper, dice, dough, dots, toy drill, dust mop, dust pan, dog, drum, doughnut box, doctor kit, dirt, diary), several objects that begin with other sounds

Place all of the **D** objects and non–**D** objects on a desk. Have the children name each object as you show it to the class. Repeat the word, emphasizing the beginning sound. As objects are named, place them on a table.

Each child comes up to the table, selects an object, and says its name. If it begins like desk, the child places it on the desk. If it does not begin like desk, he/she feeds it to the sound muncher. As a non–**D** object is eaten, the child or the class makes its beginning sound.

Leave the desk and all of the **D** objects out as a display in the classroom.

Introducing the Letter D d *(cont.)*

Letter Centers

Digging in the Dirt

Materials: pail or pan filled with dirt, a bunch of dimes, a small digger

Children dig in the dirt to see how many dimes they can find, count the dimes, and record how many they dug up.

Dozens of Fun

Materials: empty egg cartons, doughnut boxes, plastic Easter eggs, plastic doughnuts

Children count out a dozen eggs or a dozen doughnuts and place them in their appropriate containers.

Diamonds

Materials: yarn, pipe cleaners, tiny dowel rods

Cross two very small dowel rods onto an X shape. Tie the intersection with a pipe cleaner. Have the children weave multicolored yarn around the dowels to form a colorful diamond.

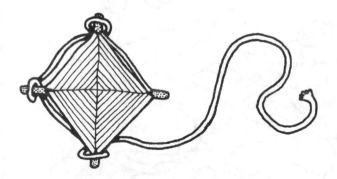

Dot to Dot

Materials: dot-to-dot pictures

Children complete dot-to-dot pictures by connecting numbers or letters of the alphabet in order.

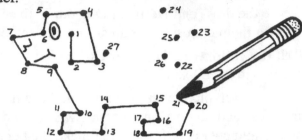

Drum

Materials: coffee cans, oatmeal boxes, drink mix containers, short pieces of dowel, decorations (yarn pieces, beads, glitters, etc.)

Children decorate their drums with a variety of materials. Give each child two dowels to use as drum sticks.

D d Play Dough

Materials: play dough, cookie cutters in shapes that begin with the letter **D** (dinosaur, dog, duck, doll, etc.)

Children press cookie cutters into the play dough to make pictures and patterns. They can also roll out the dough to form the capital and lowercase letters **D d.**

Let's Learn

Before they respond to each question or direction that you give them, ask the children to identify which word or words begin with a **D.** Write the **D** words on a wall chart or on the chalkboard.

Introducing the Letter D d *(cont.)*

Let's Learn *(cont.)*

Let's Talk

- Name something that you do daily. (brush hair, talk, eat)
- Name something that is dangerous. (fire, electric wires, some strangers)
- What is your favorite thing to drink? (water, milk, juice)
- Name something that a doctor does when you go in for a checkup. (weighs, takes temperature, looks in ears)
- Name something that a dentist does when you go in for a visit. (looks at teeth, cleans teeth, checks for cavities)
- Name an important date to remember. (birthday, Christmas, Thanksgiving)
- Name something that you can buy for one dollar. (candy, soda, pencils)

Let's Move

- Dance slowly, then fast.
- Drag your feet around the room.
- Stomp around the room like a dinosaur.
- Move around the room like a dog, deer, donkey, dragonfly, duck, dove, and/or dolphin.

Let's Pretend

Pretend to:

- do the dishes
- dig a big hole with a shovel
- dress for school

- decorate a cake
- put a leash on your dog and walk him around the room
- beat a drum

Let's Do

- Group play dollars according to their value.
- Group doll dishes according to patterns and sizes.
- Count out dots (poker or bingo chips) to correspond with oral or written numbers.
- Take a survey of favorite desserts—ice cream, cake, pie, etc. Record the data on a "Dessert Graph."
- Make up a class tongue twister using **D** words: The dirty dog dug up daises, daffodils, and dandelions.

Introducing the Letter D d *(cont.)*

Letter D Picture Cards

daisy

deer

desk

diamond

dinosaur

dishes

doctor

dog

donkey

duck

Introducing the Letter D d *(cont.)*

Patterns

Designer Dog

dress

dollar

Introducing the Letter E e

Letter E Literature: *Encore for Eleanor* by Bill Peet

Materials: crayons, paper

Show the cover of the book to the children and ask them to find the two words that start with an **E**. Talk about the meaning of the word encore. Read *Encore for Eleanor*. Discuss how the story's setting changes from the circus to the zoo. Talk about how Eleanor was happy when she was performing and, later, drawing, and how she was sad when she was not doing anything.

Have the children draw a picture of Eleanor the elephant.

What Do You Hear?

(Short and long sounds may be presented separately.)

Materials: letter **E** long and short picture cards (reproduced, colored, and laminated)

Working with one set of cards at a time, show the children each picture cards and ask them to name the object. Repeat the word, emphasizing the **E** sound, for example, e–e–e–egg. Talk about the two different sounds that the letter **E** makes. When sounding out the long **E** sound, tell the children that it says its own name, as when they say the alphabet: *E, F, G*. When sounding out the short **E** sound, tell the children that it is the beginning sound in "egg" and "every."

Give each **E** card to a child. Pick one child to come up in front of the class. That child will show the rest of the class the picture card he/she is holding. The class responds with the chant "What Do You Hear?"

Short E

Class: "Elephant, elephant, what do you hear?"
(The child in front of the class looks at the remaining pictures and calls on one.)

Child: "I hear egg beginning like me."

Class: "Egg, egg, what do you hear?"

Child: "I hear elevator beginning like me."

Continue until all of the short **E** picture cards have been called.

The last child responds "I hear the letter **E** beginning with me."

The class adds: "We all hear the short **E** sound going e–e–e–e!"

Introducing the Letter E e *(cont.)*

Long E

Class: "Ear, ear, what do you hear?" (The child in front of the class looks at the remaining pictures and calls on one.)

Child: "I hear eel beginning like me."

Class: "Eel, eel, what do you hear?"

Child: "I hear eleven beginning like me."

Continue until all of the long E picture cards have been called. The last child responds "I hear the letter E beginning with me."

The class adds: "We all hear the long E letter going e–e–e–e!"

E Is an Exciting Letter!

Materials: several large pieces of construction paper or poster board with a large capital and lowercase letter E printed on each, glue, crayons, E items: envelopes, elbow macaroni, egg shells

Divide the class into groups of four or five. Each group will glue the E items to the paper, covering the E e. When the glue dries, display the pictures on a bulletin board or wall.

Bulletin Board

Materials: crayons, markers, paper, scissors, magazines, copies of picture cards or other short and long E worksheets, glue, copies of the eel and elevator patterns for each child

Make one large copy of the eel with the following directions printed on it: *Please help decorate an electric eel with pictures that begin with the long E sound.* Make one large copy of the elevator with the following directions printed on it: *Please help decorate an elevator with pictures that begin with the short E sound.*

Staple the large eel and elevator to the bulletin board. Show the bulletin board to the children and explain the directions to them.

Have the children cut out their eels and elevators. Ask them to decorate the eels with long E pictures and the elevators with short E pictures. They can use pictures that they have drawn themselves, or pictures cut from magazines, or worksheets they have colored. Staple their finished eels and elevators to the bulletin board.

Introducing the Letter E e *(cont.)*

Sounds and Pictures

(For older or more advanced students, Short and long sounds may be presented together.)

Materials: the eagle pattern (reproduced, colored, and laminated), easel (cut a large square and legs from poster board to resemble an easel), long **E** picture cards, the elf pattern (reproduced, colored and laminated, or use a Christmas decoration), evergreen tree (cut an evergreen from green and brown poster board), short **E** picture cards, Velcro, hole punch, picture board, sound muncher

Punch a hole at the top of each picture card and hot glue a piece of Velcro to the back. Hot glue the matching Velcro pieces to the easel or the evergreen.

Mix the long and short **E** picture cards and hang them on the picture board.

Hang the easel and the evergreen on the wall where the children can see and touch them. Place the elf by the evergreen and the eagle by the easel.

Gather the children by the eagle, easel, elf, evergreen tree, and picture board.

Short E

Tell the children: "I would like you to meet Mr. Elf. Mr. Elf is very sad because nobody visits him at his home in the evergreen forest. He is so lonely that he cries ě–ě–ě–ě all day long. (Have the children make the ě–ě–ě–ě sound like Mr. Elf does.) Mr. Elf thinks that if he decorates his evergreen tree with exciting pictures that begin with the short E sound, other elves will see his evergreen tree and visit him so he will not be lonely anymore. Can you help Mr. Elf decorate his evergreen with exciting pictures that begin with the same sound as elf, evergreen, and the sound of Mr. Elf crying ě–ě–ě–ě?"

As you point to each picture on the board, the children name the object. Repeat the word, emphasizing the beginning sound of each picture. Call the children one at a time to come up to the picture board and pick out a card. If the picture begins with a short **E** sound, he/she sticks it on the evergreen. Have Mr. Elf and the children make the short ě–ě–ě–ě sound each time a new short **E** picture is added to the evergreen.

Introducing the Letter E e *(cont.)*

Sounds and Pictures *(cont.)*

Long E

Tell the children: "Mr. Eagle is also visiting. Mr. Eagle is a very special eagle because he can paint wonderful pictures on his easel. Whenever he paints a picture, he makes a certain ē–ē–ē–ē sound. (Have the children pretend to paint a picture on an easel and make the ē–ē–ē–ē sound like Mr. Eagle does.)

Mr. Eagle has brought his easel with him today because he wants to start painting pictures of things that start with the long E sound. Can you help Mr. Eagle decorate his easel with pictures that start with the same sound as eagle, easel, and the ē–ē–ē–ē sound that he makes when he paints a picture?"

As you point to each picture on the board, the children name the object. Repeat the word, emphasizing the beginning sound of each picture. Call the children one at a time to come up to the picture board and pick out a card. If it begins with a long E, the child sticks it on the easel while Mr. Eagle and the children make the long sound. Leave the easel, eagle, evergreen, and elf on display in the classroom.

After you have done this activity a few times, mix up the pictures on the easel and the evergreen.

Tell the children: "Mr. Eagle flew by the easel and the evergreen and accidentally knocked all of the picture cards off the wall. The pictures got all mixed up, so he tried to put them back in their proper places, but he is not sure if he put them back correctly."

Ask the children to look at the easel and the evergreen and identify any pictures which need to be changed from the long E easel to the short E evergreen or vice versa.

To challenge your class even more, add some non–E picture cards on both the easel and the evergreen. Tell the children that the E pictures were mixed up with the other picture cards. When the children find a non–E picture card on the easel or the evergreen, have them feed it to the sound muncher. The sound muncher and the children make the sound of the non–E picture as it is being eaten.

Introducing the Letter E e *(cont.)*

Sounds and Objects

Long E

Materials: eleven (write the number 11 on a large piece of construction paper), objects that begin with the long **E** sound (Easter basket, Easter bunny, eagle, eraser, map with east circled)

Short E

Materials: exit sign (write the word EXIT on a large piece of construction paper), objects that begin with the short **E** sound (egg carton, egg, elephant, evergreen branch, envelopes)

Place all of the E objects on the eleven and EXIT sign on the floor. Have the children name each object as you show it to the class. Repeat the word, emphasizing the long or short sound at the beginning. As the objects are named, place them on a table.

Each child comes up to the table, selects an object, and says its name. If it begins like eleven, the child places it on the number eleven. If it begins like exit, he/she places it on the exit sign.

When you feel that the children can distinguish between the long and short **E** sounds, you might like to challenge them by adding into the group objects that begin with other sounds.

If a child picks up one of these objects, he/she can feed it to the sound muncher. As a non–**E** item is eaten, the child or the class makes its beginning sound.

Letter Centers

Food I Like to Eat

Materials: pictures of food from grocery store advertisements, crayons, markers, glue, scissors, paper

Children cut out and color foods that they like to eat. Have them write at the top of the paper: Food I Like to Eat.

Exciting Eggs

Materials: colored foam meat trays cut in small pieces, paper, glue, markers

Children draw ovals on their papers and decorate the insides of their eggs with "egg shells" (cut up foam trays) and markers.

E e Play Dough

Materials: play dough, cookie cutters in shapes that begin with the long and short letter **E** (elephant, egg, eagle, ear, etc.)

Children press cookie cutters into the play dough to make pictures and patterns. They can also roll out the dough to form the capital and lowercase letters **E e**.

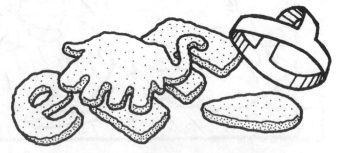

Introducing the Letter E e *(cont.)*

Let's Learn

Have the children tell you which word or words begin with a long or short **E** sound in each question or command that you read to them. Write the long and short **E** words on a wall chart or on the chalkboard.

Let's Talk

- Name something that you might see in the evening. (stars, fireflies, moon, headlights)
- Name something that is enormous. (elephant, building in the city, tree, mountain)
- Name a place where you would see an exit sign. (movie theater, office building, store, school)
- Name something that you do at Easter. (go to church, hunt for eggs, eat at Grandma's house)

Let's Move

- Move your right and left elbows up and down and then in forward and backward circles.
- Move around the room like an elephant, eagle, and eel.

Let's Pretend

Pretend to:

- break, scramble, and eat an egg
- ride an elephant
- decorate Easter eggs
- look over the edge of a cliff
- get on an elevator and ride to the eleventh floor

Let's Do

- Count elbow macaroni out to correspond with oral or written numbers.
- Take a class survey of favorite ways to eat eggs: scrambled, fried, poached, sunny-side up, etc. Record the results on an "Egg Graph."
- Make up a class tongue twister using long **E** words: *The eagle eats an enormous meal at eleven on Easter.*
- Make up a class tongue twister using short **E** words: *The Eskimo exits from the elevator on every floor.*

• SCRAMBLED	AMY	JASON	ROBBY	NANCY	VINNIE	
• FRIED	JOE	KIM	WANDA			
• POACHED	BRENDA					
• RAW						
• SUNNY-SIDE UP	MURPHY	ANNIE	TARA	DAVID	STEVE	CINDY
• OVER EASY	DANA	MORGAN	PETE	LUCY		
• EGGS? YUCK!	RANDY	ELLIE				

Introducing the Letter E e *(cont.)*

Long E Picture Cards

eagle

equal

easel

east

Easter

eel

eat

eleven

eraser

electricity

48

Introducing the Letter E e *(cont.)*

Short E Picture Cards

egg

elbow

elephant

elevator

elf

elm

Eskimo

evergreen

EXIT

exit

empty

Introducing the Letter E e *(cont.)*

Patterns

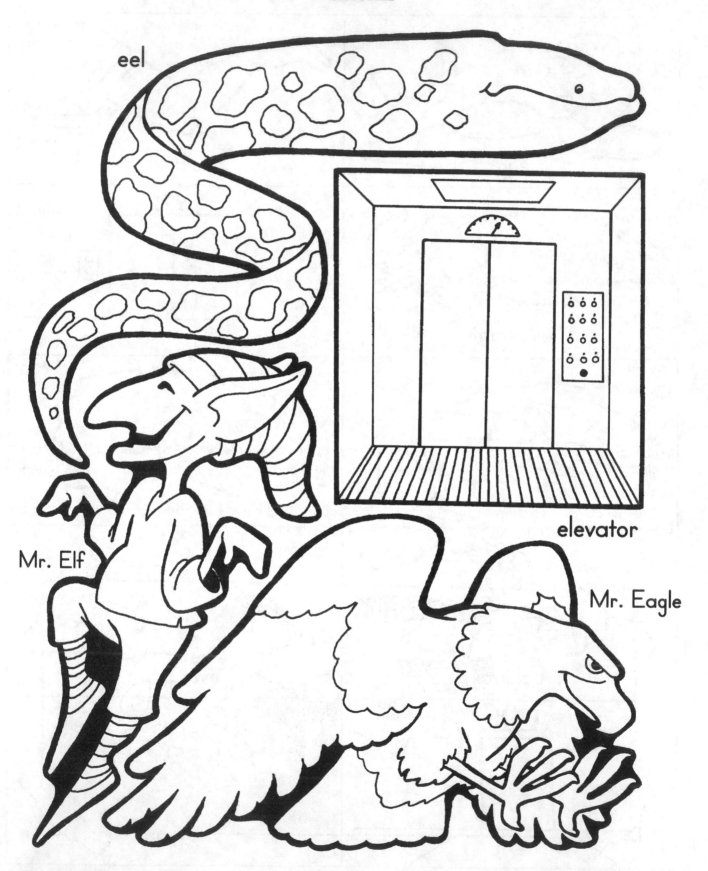

eel

elevator

Mr. Elf

Mr. Eagle

Introducing the Letter F f

Letter F Literature: *The Foot Book* by Dr. Seuss

Materials: construction paper

After reading *The Foot Book* to the children, talk about all the different kinds of feet mentioned in the story. Trace the children's feet on construction paper. The children cut out the outlines and write their names *(Ashlee's Feet)* on their feet. Glue all the feet inside a huge footprint or letter **F**.

What Do You Hear?

Materials: letter **F** picture cards (reproduced, colored, and laminated)

Talk about the sound that the letter **F** makes. Show the children each of the picture cards and ask them to identify each picture. Repeat the word, emphasizing the **F** sound.

Give each card to a child. Pick one child to come up in front of the class. That child will show the rest of the class the picture card he/she is holding. The class responds with the chant "What Do You Hear?"

Class: "Fish, fish, what do you hear?" (The child in front of the class looks at the remaining pictures and calls on one.)

Child: "I hear fire beginning like me."

Class: "Fire, fire, what do you hear?"

Child: "I hear fox beginning like me."

Continue until all the picture cards have been called. The last child responds: "I hear the letter **F** beginning with me."

The class adds: "We all hear the **F** sound going f–f–f–f!"

F Is a Fantastic Letter!

Materials: several large pieces of construction paper or poster board with a large capital and lowercase **F** printed on them, glue, **F** items (felt pieces, feathers, coffee filters, flowers, plastic forks, foil, fabric, fish-shaped crackers)

Divide the class into groups of four or five. Each group will glue the **F** items to the paper, covering the **F f**. When the glue dries, display the pictures on a bulletin board or wall.

Introducing the Letter F f *(cont.)*

Bulletin Board

Materials: crayons or markers: paper, scissors, magazines, copies of picture cards or other **F** worksheets, glue, one copy of the fish pattern for each child

Make one large fish. Print the following directions on the fish: *Please help fill a fancy fish with fantastic pictures that begin with the letter* **F**.

Staple the large fish in the center of the bulletin board. Show the bulletin board to the children and explain the directions to them.

Have the children cut out their fish and decorate it with pictures that begin with the letter **F**. They can use pictures that they have drawn themselves, pictures cut from magazines and pictures from worksheets they have colored. Staple their finished fish to the bulletin board.

The children can search at home for additional **F** pictures to be added to the bulletin board.

Sounds and Pictures

Materials: frog (use a stuffed one or a reproduced, colored, and laminated frog pattern), a felt flag, **F** picture cards, some non–**F** picture cards, Velcro, hole punch, picture board, sound muncher

Punch a hole at the top of each picture card and hot glue a Velcro piece on the back. Hot glue the matching Velcro pieces to the flag.

Place most of the **F** picture cards and some non–**F** picture cards on the picture board. Save a few **F** picture cards and several non–**F** picture cards to be added later.

Hang the flag on the wall where the children can touch and look at it. Place the frog near the flag. Gather the children by the flag, fox, picture board, and sound muncher.

Tell the children: "I would like you to meet Friendly Frog. Friendly Frog is different from other frogs because he makes a special sound. Instead of saying "ribbit, ribbit," he makes f–f–f–f sound. (Have the children make the f–f–f–f sound like Friendly.) He has brought his felt flag with him today because he needs our help. He wants his felt flag to be decorated with fun, fantastic, fabulous pictures that start with the letter **F**. Can you help him decorate his flag with pictures that start with the same sound as frog, flag, and the special sound that he makes, f–f–f–f?"

Introducing the Letter F f *(cont.)*

Sounds and Pictures *(cont.)*

As you point to each picture on the picture board, have the children name the object. Repeat each word, emphasizing the beginning sound of each picture card. Call the children one at a time to come up to the picture board and pick out a card. If it begins with an **F**, the child sticks it on the flag while Friendly Frog and the children make his special sound, f–f–f–f. If it does not begin with an **F**, he/she feeds it to the sound muncher. Have the child or the class make the beginning sound of the non–**F** picture as it is being eaten.

Leave the flag and frog out in the classroom. After you have done this activity several times, mix up the pictures on the flag and add some more **F** pictures and several non–**F** pictures to the flag.

Tell the children: "Friendly Frog added some more pictures to his flag, but he is not sure if they all begin with the **F** sound."

Point to each picture and have the class say the word with you. Ask the children to look at the flag and identify any pictures which need to be removed and fed to the sound muncher. Have the sound muncher and the children make the beginning sound of the non–**F** picture as it is being eaten.

Sounds and Objects

Materials: large piece of fabric, objects that begin with the letter **F** (feathers, film box, coffee filter, flowers, bag of flour, fork, fuse, French fry container, flag, flashlight, felt, fig bars, frosting container, fan, fruit), several objects that begin with other sounds

Place the fabric on the floor. Place all of the **F** objects and non–**F** objects on top of the fabric. Have the children name each object as you show it to the class. Repeat the word, emphasizing the beginning sound. As objects are named, place them on a table.

Each child comes up to the table, selects an object, and says its name. If it begins like fabric, the child places it on the fabric. If it does not begin like fabric, he/she feeds it to the sound muncher. The child or the class makes the sound of the non–**F** object as the object is being eaten.

Leave the fabric and all of the **F** objects out as a display in the classroom.

Introducing the Letter F f *(cont.)*

Letter Centers

Fruity Fragrances

Materials: glue, flavored gelatin or drink mix, outlines of fruit

Children trace pieces of fruit with glue, sprinkle with corresponding flavored powdered mix over the glue, shake off extra mix, and let it dry.

Fruity Necklaces

Materials: yarn, fruit flavored cereal

Children string yarn through holes in the fruit cereal, hang necklaces around their necks and eat them like candy necklaces.

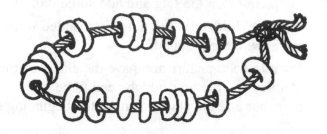

F f Play Dough

Materials: play dough, plastic forks, cookie cutters with pictures that begin with the letter **F** (feather, fish, farm, fruit, etc.)

Children press forks and cookie cutters into the play dough to make pictures and patterns. They can also roll the dough to form the capital and lowercase letters **F f.**

Felt Pictures

Materials: pieces of felt in various sizes and colors, glue, paper

Children glue down felt pieces to make a picture.

Gone Fishing

Materials: round, shallow container, construction paper fish, paper clips, ruler, magnets, yarn

Print uppercase and/or lowercase **F**'s on most of the fish and other letters on the rest. Laminate the fish and glue magnetic strips on the backs. Tie one end of yarn to a ruler and fasten a paper clip at the other end to resemble a fishing pole.

Children go fishing with a partner and try to catch as many fish as they can. The child with the most **F f** fish wins.

Let's Learn

Have the children tell you which word or words begin with an **F** in each question or command that you read to them. Write the **F** words out on a chart or on the chalkboard.

Introducing the Letter F f *(cont.)*

Let's Learn *(cont.)*

Let's Talk

- Name something that you can fold. (laundry, paper, napkins, table)
- Name something that you eat frozen. (ice-cream, Popsicle, sherbet, candy bar)
- Name something that is fun to do. (ride a bike, jump rope, read, play with friends)
- Name different kinds of furniture. (chair, bed, table, sofa)
- Name something that is fuzzy. (coat, stuffed animals, mitten)
- Name an animal that has fur. (dog, cat, raccoon, bear)
- Name a type of fruit. (orange, apple, grapes, banana)
- Name a type of fish. (cod, flounder, bass, carp)
- Name something that you would see in the fall season. (falling leaves, pumpkins, football games)
- Name something that you might see on a farm. (barn, fence, cows, chickens)

Let's Move

- Swim around the room like a fish.
- Hop around the room like a frog.
- Move around the room like a fox.
- Show me what you would do in the case of a fire (stop, drop, and roll).

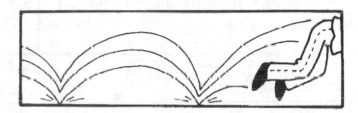

Let's Pretend

Pretend to:

- catch a fish
- fold the laundry
- polish the furniture

- wash your face and feet
- eat French fries (don't forget to dip them into ketchup)

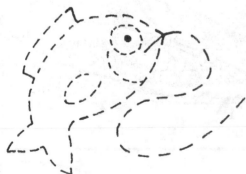

Let's Do

- Group felt pieces according to size and/or color.
- Count fish-shaped crackers to correspond with oral or written numbers.
- Take a survey of favorite fruits and create a "Fruit Graph."
- Make up a class tongue twister using F words: *Friendly Farmer found four frogs and five foxes on his farm on Friday.*

Introducing the Letter F f *(cont.)*

Letter F Picture Cards

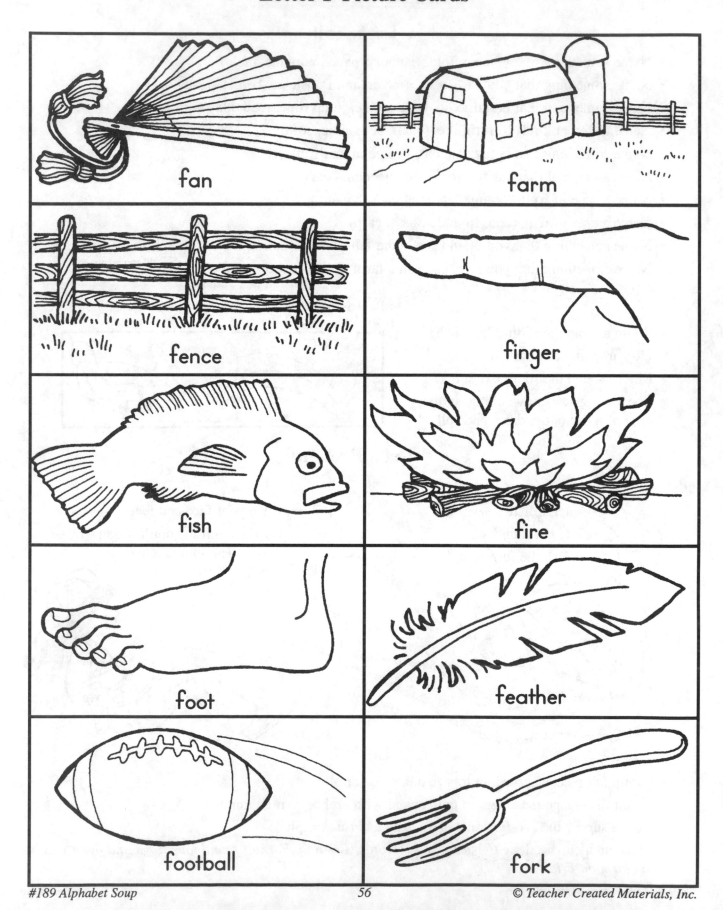

fan

farm

fence

finger

fish

fire

foot

feather

football

fork

56

Introducing the Letter F f *(cont.)*

Patterns

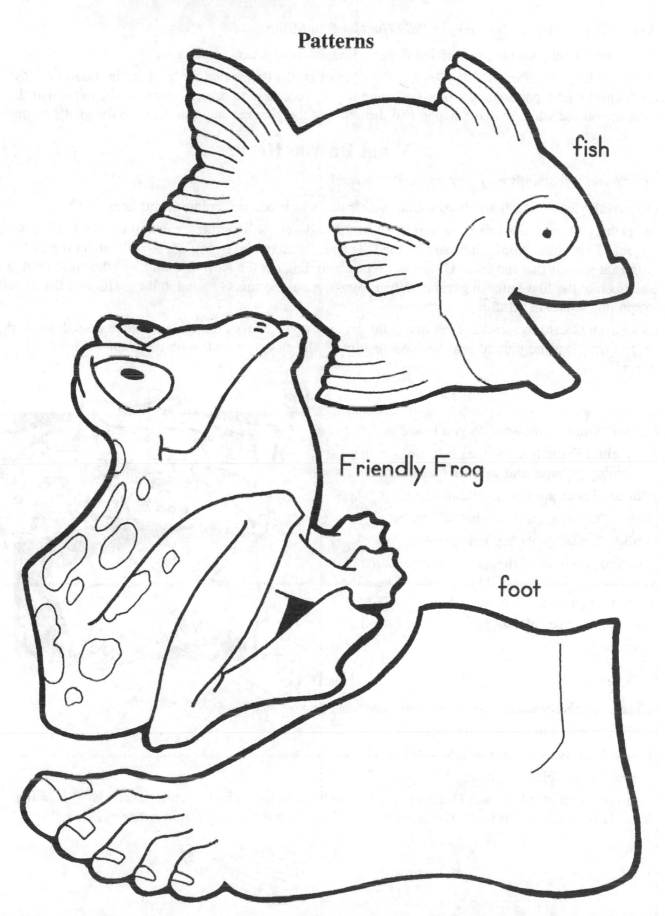

fish

Friendly Frog

foot

Introducing the Letter G g

Letter G Literature: *The Hungry Billy Goat* by Rita Milios

Materials: goat pattern, construction paper, white drawing paper, crayons

After reading *The Hungry Billy Goat*, make a list of all the things that the goat ate in the story. Give each child a goat pattern and a piece of white paper. Ask them to draw pictures of the items that the goat ate on the white drawing paper, and then cut out the pictures and glue them to the goat's stomach.

What Do You Hear?

(Hard and soft sounds may be presented separately.)

Materials: letter **G** soft and hard sound picture cards (reproduced, colored, and laminated)

Working with one set of cards at a time, show the children each picture card, and ask them to name the object. Repeat the word, emphasizing the **G** sound, for example, g–g–g–gate. Talk about the two different sounds that the letter **G** makes. When sounding out the hard **G** sound, tell the children that it sounds like the first letter in gorilla. When sounding out the soft **G** sound, tell the children that it is the beginning sound in giraffe.

Give each **G** card to a child. Pick one child to come up in front of the class. That child will show the rest of the class the picture card he/she is holding. The class responds with the chant "What Do You Hear?"

Hard G

Class: "Gum, gum, what do you hear?"

(The child in the front of the class looks at the remaining pictures and calls on one.)

Child: "I hear garden beginning like me."

Class: "Garden, garden, what do you hear?"

Child: "I hear ghost beginning like me."

Continue until all of the hard **G** picture cards have been called. The last child responds: "I hear the letter **G** beginning with me."

The class adds: "We all hear the hard **G** going g–g–g–g."

Soft G

Class: "Gingerbread man, gingerbread man, what do you hear?"

Child: "I hear giraffe beginning like me."

Class: "Giraffe, giraffe, what do you hear?"

Child: "I hear giant beginning like me."

Continue until all of the soft **G** picture cards have been called. The last child responds: "I hear the letter **G** beginning with me." The class adds: "We all hear the soft **G** sound going g–g–g–g!"

Introducing the Letter G g *(cont.)*

G Is a Great Letter!

Materials: several large pieces of construction paper or poster board with a large capital and lowercase **G** printed on each, glue, **G** items (gum wrappers, graham crackers, gingersnaps, glue, gummy bears, gelatin containers, gold and green glitter, gauze, grass, gravel)

Divide the class into groups of four or five. The children work together to glue the **G** items on top of the **G g**. When the glue dries, display the pictures on a bulletin board or a wall.

Bulletin Board

Materials: crayons, markers, scissors, magazines, copies of picture cards or other hard and soft **G** worksheets, glue, aluminum foil, copies of the gum wrapper and gingersnap pattern for each child

Make one large copy of the gum wrapper and glue aluminum foil strips on the ends. Write the following directions on the wrapper: *Please help decorate a gum wrapper with gorgeous pictures that begin with the hard G sound.*

Make one large copy of the gingersnap and write the following directions on it: *Please help decorate a gingersnap with pictures that begin with the soft G sound.*

Staple the wrapper and gingersnap to the bulletin board. Show the bulletin board to the children and explain the directions.

Have the children cut out their gingersnaps and gum wrappers and glue the aluminum foil to the ends of the gum wrappers. Have them decorate the gingersnaps with soft **G** pictures and the gum wrappers with hard **G** pictures, using pictures that they have drawn, pictures cut from magazines, or worksheets they have colored. Staple their finished gingersnaps and gum wrappers onto the bulletin board.

The children can search at home for additional **G** pictures to be added to the bulletin board.

Sounds and Pictures

(For older or more advanced students, hard and soft sounds may be presented together.)

Materials: the gingerbread man and ghost patterns (copied, colored, and laminated), hard and soft **G** picture cards, Velcro, hole punch, picture board, sound muncher

Punch a hole at the top of each hard and soft **G** picture card and hot glue a Velcro piece to the back. Hot glue the matching Velcro piece to the gingerbread man or the ghost.

Introducing the Letter G g *(cont.)*

Sounds and Pictures *(cont.)*

Hang the gingerbread man and ghost on the wall where the children can see and touch them. Gather the children by the gingerbread man, ghost, picture board, and sound muncher.

Hard G

Tell the children: "I would like you to meet Mrs. Ghost. Mrs. Ghost is a good, friendly ghost and a great gardener. You can hear her out in her garden making a special g–g–g–g sound as she works. (Have the children pretend to work in a garden while making the hard g–g–g–g sound.) Mrs. Ghost stays in her greenhouse most of the time because she does not want people to be frightened of her ghostly appearance. She does not want people to be scared of her anymore. She thinks that if she was decorated in gorgeous pictures that start with the hard **G** sound, people wouldn't be frightened away. Can you help decorate her with pictures that start with the same sound that you hear at the beginning of ghost, garden, and the special sound she makes, g–g–g–g?"

Point to each picture on the picture board as the children tell you what is on each card. Repeat each word, emphasizing the beginning sound of each picture card. Call the children one at a time to come up to the picture board and pick out a card. If it begins with a hard **G**, the child sticks it on Mrs. Ghost while Mrs. Ghost and the children make the hard g–g–g–g sound.

Soft G

Tell the children: "Mr. Gingerbread is visiting today. Mr. Gingerbread is here today because he does not want to be eaten. He is being chased by everybody who sees him. He makes a special g–g–g–g sound as he runs away in his gym shoes from anyone who tries to eat him. (Have the children pretend to run while making the soft g–g–g–g sound like Mr. Gingerbread does.) Mr. Gingerbread thinks that if he is decorated with pictures that begin with the soft **G** sound that people will leave him alone and stop trying to eat him up. Can you help decorate him with pictures that start with the same sound that you hear at the beginning of gingerbread, gym shoes, and the special sound he makes as he runs, g–g–g–g?"

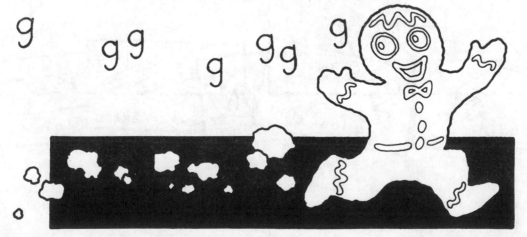

Introducing the Letter G g *(cont.)*

Sounds and Pictures *(cont.)*

Point to each picture on the picture board as the children tell you what is on each card. Repeat each word, emphasizing the beginning sound of each picture card. Call the children one at a time to come up to the picture board and pick out a card. If it begins with a soft **G**, the child sticks it to Mr. Gingerbread and makes the soft g–g–g–g sound. Leave the ghost and the gingerbread man out in the classroom.

After you have done this activity several times, mix up the pictures.

Tell the children: "A gust of wind blew through the room last night and all of the pictures fell off. Mr. Gingerbread and Mrs. Ghost tried to stick all of the pictures back in the right spot, but they are not sure if they put them back correctly."

Ask the children to look at the ghost and the gingerbread man and identify any pictures which need to be changed from the ghost to the gingerbread man and vice versa.

If you want to challenge your class even more, stick some non–G picture cards on the Mrs. Ghost and Mr. Gingerbread. Tell the children that the **G** pictures were mixed up with other picture cards. When the children find a non–G picture card, have them feed it to the sound muncher. The child or the class makes the beginning sound of the non–G picture as it is being eaten.

Sounds and Objects

Hard G

Materials: garbage can, objects that begin with the hard letter **G** (empty gallon jugs, gauze, gift, glasses, glitter, globe, glove, glue, golf ball, gourd, grass, gravel, gum, garlic)

Soft G

Materials: gym shoes, objects that begin with the soft letter **G** (gingersnaps, gingerbread, ginger ale, ginger-spice, gelatin, toy giraffe)

Arrange the garbage can and gym shoes on the floor. Put the hard and soft **G** objects in the garbage can. Remove them one by one and show each one to the class. Have the children name each object. Repeat the word, emphasizing the beginning sound. As objects are named, place them on a table.

Each child comes up to the table, selects an object, and says its name. If it begins like gym, the child places it by the pair of gym shoes. If it begins like garbage, the child puts it in the garbage can.

Introducing the Letter G g *(cont.)*

Sounds and Objects *(cont.)*

Anytime you feel that the children can distinguish between the hard and soft **G** sounds, you may decide to challenge them by adding into the group objects that begin with other sounds. If a child picks up one of these non–**G** objects he/she can feed it to the sound muncher. Have the child or the class make the beginning sound of the non–**G** object as it is being eaten.

Leave the garbage can and the gym shoes and all of the **G** items out as a display in the classroom.

Letter Centers

Gravel

Materials: pan filled with gravel, shovels, **G** objects (golf balls, glue sticks, green crayons, graph, etc.)

Children shovel and dig in the gravel to find gum balls, golf balls, and glue sticks. Sort and count objects and record on a bar graph.

G g Play Dough

Materials: green and grape (purple) play dough, golf balls, gravel, cookie cutters with pictures that begin with the hard or soft **G** sound (ghost, giraffe, goat, etc.)

Children press golf balls, gravel, and cookie cutters into the play dough to make pictures and patterns. They can also roll out the dough to form the capital and lowercase letters **G g**.

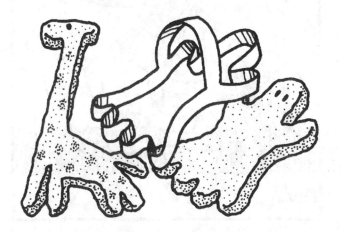

Gym

Materials: paper, markers, crayons, craft sticks, toothpicks, glue

Children design their own outside play gym.

Green Things

Materials: green paint, markers, crayons, coloring sheets of green things (frogs, grasshoppers, watermelons, etc.)

Children color, paint or draw pictures of green things.

G Prints

Materials: glove, gauze, golf ball, gravel, green paint, paper

Children dip **G** items into the green paint and press onto paper to make **G** prints.

Let's Learn

Before they respond to each question or direction that you give them, ask the children to identify which word or words begin with a **G**. Write the **G** words on a wall chart or on the chalkboard.

Introducing the Letter G g *(cont.)*

Let's Learn *(cont.)*

Let's Talk

- Name something that is green. (grass, grapes, frogs)
- Name something that you might see in a garden. (tomatoes, watermelon, rabbits, bugs)
- Name something that is gooey. (gum, cookie dough, glue)
- Name something that you might see in a gym. (mats, weights, treadmill)
- Name a flavor of gum. (grape, spearmint, strawberry)
- Name something that you buy by the gallon. (milk, orange juice, gas, kerosene, water)
- Name something that you like to do with your grandparents. (read, talk, play games)
- What is your favorite game to play outside? (kickball, hide and seek, softball)
- Name a food that you like to put gravy on. (mashed potatoes, biscuits, meat)

Let's Move

- Gallop across the room.
- Glide across the room.
- Walk as though the room is full of something gooey.
- Move around the room like a giant, a goat, a gorilla, and a goose.

Let's Pretend

Pretend to:

- put on gloves, goggles and galoshes
- wrap a gigantic gift
- play golf
- play the guitar

Let's Do

- Count out gummy bears to correspond with oral or written numbers.
- Open a bag of colored gum balls. Have the children group gum balls according to color, count each group, and record results on a "Gum Ball Graph."
- Make up a class tongue twister using hard **G** words: *The grasshopper found gold, glitter, glass, gravel, and a gourd in his garden.*
- Make up a class tongue twister using soft **G** words: *The giant giraffe ate gingersnaps in the gym.*

Introducing the Letter G g *(cont.)*

Hard G Picture Cards

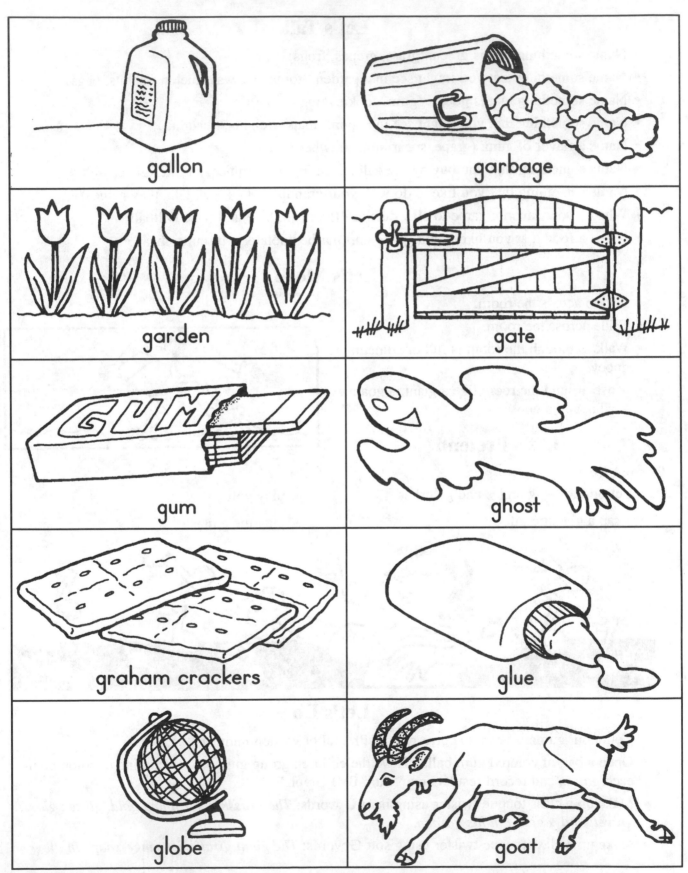

gallon

garbage

garden

gate

gum

ghost

graham crackers

glue

globe

goat

Introducing the Letter G g *(cont.)*

Soft G Picture Cards

gelatin

gem

giraffe

gingerbread man

ginger ale

gymnast

giant

Introducing the Letter G g *(cont.)*

Patterns

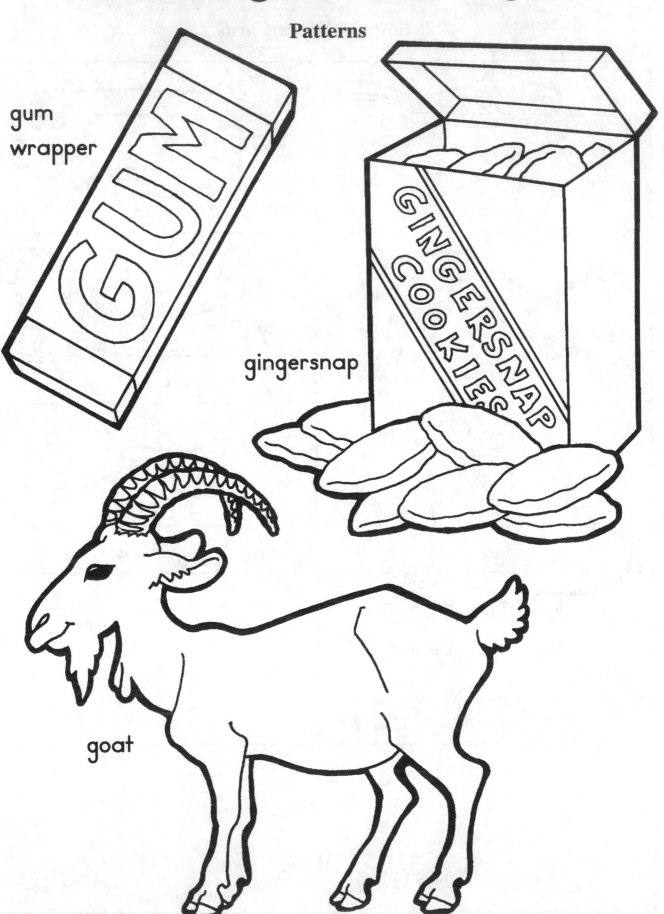

gum wrapper

gingersnap

goat

66

Introducing the Letter G g *(cont.)*

Patterns *(cont.)*

Mr. Gingerbread

Mrs. Ghost

Introducing the Letter H h

Letter H Literature: *The Real Hole* by Beverly Cleary

Materials: construction paper, crayons

After reading *The Real Hole*, discuss the many ideas people in the story had for the hole: a nest, a place to catch fish, a place for baby rabbits to live, bury bones in it, and plant a tree. Have the children draw a hole on their papers and then add a picture of something that they would like to fill the hole with.

What Do You Hear?

Materials: letter **H** picture cards (reproduced, colored, and laminated)

Talk about the sound that the letter **H** makes. Show the children each of the picture cards and ask them to name each object. Repeat the word, emphasizing the **H** sound.

Give each card to a child. Pick one child to come up in front of the class. That child will show the rest of the class the picture card he/she is holding. The class responds with the chant "What Do You Hear?"

Class: "Horse, horse, what do you hear?" (The child in the front of the class looks at the remaining pictures and calls on one.)

Child: "I hear hamburger beginning like me."

Class: "Hamburger, hamburger, what do you hear?"

Child: "I hear hammer beginning like me."

Continue until all of the picture cards have been called. The last child responds: "I hear the letter **H** beginning with me."

The class adds: "We all hear the **H** sound going h–h–h–h!"

H Is a Happy Letter!

Materials: large pieces of construction paper or poster board with a large capital and lowercase **H** printed on each, glue, **H** items (heart-shaped candy, hooks, panty hose, pieces cut from an old garden hose, hamburger wrappers, hangers)

Divide the class into groups of four or five. The children work together to glue the **H** items on the **H h**. When the glue dries, display the pictures on a bulletin board or a wall.

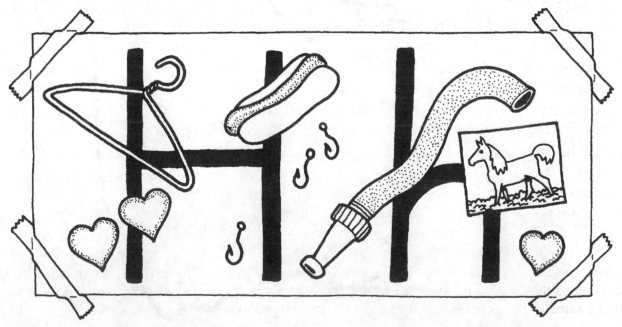

Introducing the Letter H h *(cont.)*

Bulletin Board

Materials: crayons, markers, paper, scissors, magazines, copies of picture cards or other **H** worksheets, glue, copies of the hand pattern for each child

Make one large copy of the hand and write the following directions on it: Please be helpful and fill the hands with happy pictures that begin with the letter **H**.

Staple the large hand in the center of the bulletin board. Show the bulletin board to the children and explain the directions to them.

Give each child a copy of the hand or trace each child's hand on paper. Ask the children to cut out and decorate their hands with pictures that begin with the letter H, using pictures that they have drawn, pictures cut from magazines, or worksheets that they have colored. Staple their finished hands to the bulletin board.

The children can search at home for additional pictures that begin with **H** to add to the bulletin board.

Sounds and Pictures

Materials: horse (use a stuffed one or a reproduced, colored, and laminated horse pattern), haystack (yellow or light brown paper, laminated and cut in the shape of a haystack), **H** picture cards, several non–**H** picture cards, Velcro, picture board, sound muncher

Punch a hole near the top of each picture card and hot glue a piece of Velcro to the back. Hot glue the matching Velcro pieces to the haystack.

Place most of the **H** picture cards and some non–**H** picture cards on the picture board. Save a few **H** picture cards and several non–**H** picture cards to be added later.

Hang the haystack on the wall where the children can touch and look at it. Place the horse by the haystack.

Gather the children by the horse, haystack, picture board, and sound muncher.

Tell the children: "I would like you to meet Hungry Horse. Hungry Horse is different from other horses because instead of making a neigh, neigh sound, he makes an h–h–h–h sound whenever he is hungry. (Have the children make the sound that Hungry Horse makes when he is hungry h–h–h–h.) Hungry Horse is here today because he needs our help. He wants us to help him decorate his haystack with pictures that begin with the letter **H**. Can you help him fill his haystack with pictures that start with the same sound as horse, haystack, and the special sound that he makes, h–h–h–h?"

Introducing the Letter H h *(cont.)*

Sounds and Pictures *(cont.)*

As you point to each picture on the board, the children name the object. Repeat the word, emphasizing the beginning sound of each picture card. Call the children one at a time to come up to the picture board and pick out a card. If it begins with an **H**, the child sticks it on the haystack while Hungry Horse and the children make the special h–h–h–h sound. If it does not begin with an **H**, he/she feeds it to the sound muncher. The child or the class makes the appropriate beginning sound while the picture is being eaten.

Leave the haystack and Hungry Horse out in the classroom. After you have done this activity several times, mix up the pictures on the haystack and add some more H pictures and several non–**H** pictures to the haystack.

Tell the children: "Hungry Horse added some more pictures to his haystack, but he is not sure if they all begin with the **H** sound."

Point to each picture on the haystack and have the class say the word with you. Ask the children to look at the haystack and identify the pictures that need to be removed and fed to the sound muncher. Have the sound muncher and the children make the beginning sound of the non–**H** picture as it is being eaten.

Sounds and Objects

Materials: garden hose, objects that begin with the letter **H** (hair spray, hamburger wrapper, hair bow, headband, hula hoop, hammer, handle, helmet, honey, horn, toy handcuffs, hat, harmonica, toy hatchet, hay, hazelnut, hangers, headphones, toy helicopter), several objects that begin with other sounds

Make a big circle with a garden hose on the floor. Place all of the **H** and non–**H** objects inside the hose circle. Have the children name each object as you show it to the class. Repeat the word, emphasizing the beginning sound. As objects are named, place them on a table.

Each child comes up to the table, selects an object, and says its name. If it begins like hose, the child places it on the hose. If it does not begin like hose, he/she feeds it to the sound muncher. As non–**H** objects are eaten, the child or the class makes its beginning sound.

Leave the hose and all of the **H** objects out as a display in the classroom.

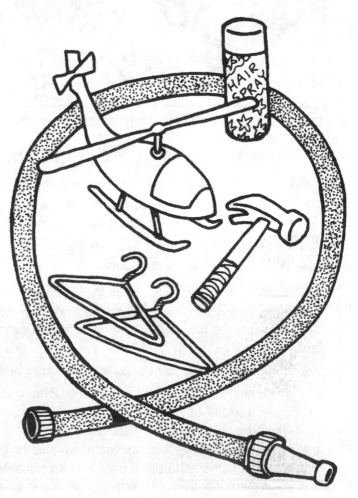

Introducing the Letter H h *(cont.)*

Letter Centers

Helping at Home

Materials: paper, crayons, markers

Children draw pictures of their home and of things that they do to help around home.

Hook a Halibut

Materials: laminated paper fish shapes, hot glue gun, rulers or paint stirrers, string or yarn

Write **H h** on most of the fish and different letters of the alphabet on the remainder. Glue small pieces of strip magnets on the back of each fish. Attach one end of string to a ruler, and tie a paper clip to the opposite end.

Turn the fish over so that the letters of the alphabet do not show and mix the fish up.

Children take turns catching the halibut. The child who catches the most halibut (**H h** fish) wins.

H h Play Dough

Materials: play dough, cookie cutters in shapes that begin with the letter **H** (house, horse, heart, hat, etc.)

Children press cookie cutters into the play dough to make patterns. They can also roll the dough to form the capital and lowercase letters **H h**.

Half H Pictures

Materials: pictures of objects that begin with the letter **H** (house, head, horse, helicopter, etc.) cut in half, paper, glue, pencils

Children select a half picture, glue it to a piece of paper and complete the other half of the **H** picture.

Let's Learn

Before they respond to each question or direction that you give them, ask the children to identify which word or words begin with an **H**. Write the **H** words on a wall chart or on the chalkboard.

Introducing the Letter H h *(cont.)*

Let's Learn *(cont.)*

Let's Talk

- Name something that you would need to wash your hair. (shampoo, conditioner, towel)
- Name something that is or can get hot. (water, stove, iron)
- Name something that you needed help to do when you were little, but now you can do all by yourself. (eat, get dressed, take a bath)
- Name a body part that begins with the letter **H**. (heart, heel, head, hair, hip)
- Name something that is a bad habit. (smoking, nail biting, spitting)
- Name something that makes you happy. (treats, family, friends)
- Tell what honey feels and tastes like and what you like to put it on. (sticky, gooey, sweet; on biscuits, bread)
- What does it mean to be handicapped?
- What can you do to keep healthy? (eat good food, exercise, see doctor)
- When would you need to wear a helmet? (skateboarding, bike riding, playing football, etc.)

Let's Move

- Hop: forwards, backwards, and sideways.
- Move around the room like a hippopotamus, horse, hamster, hog, hyena.
- Fly around the room like a hawk and a hummingbird.
- Walk around the room on the heels of your feet.

Let's Pretend

Pretend to:

- hammer a nail into the wall and hang a picture
- make a hamburger and eat it
- play the harp, a horn, a harmonica
- put on a hat, helmet

- dig a hole
- look down from a high place
- fly a helicopter
- wash, dry, and brush your hair

Let's Do

Group children according to hair color (black, brown, blonde, and red), texture (straight or curly), lengths (short, medium, or long).

Count heart-shaped candy to correspond with oral or written numbers.

Make up a class tongue twister using **H** words: *Hungry Horse had huge helpings of hay, hamburgers, hot dogs, and honey.*

Introducing the Letter H h (cont.)

Letter H Picture Cards

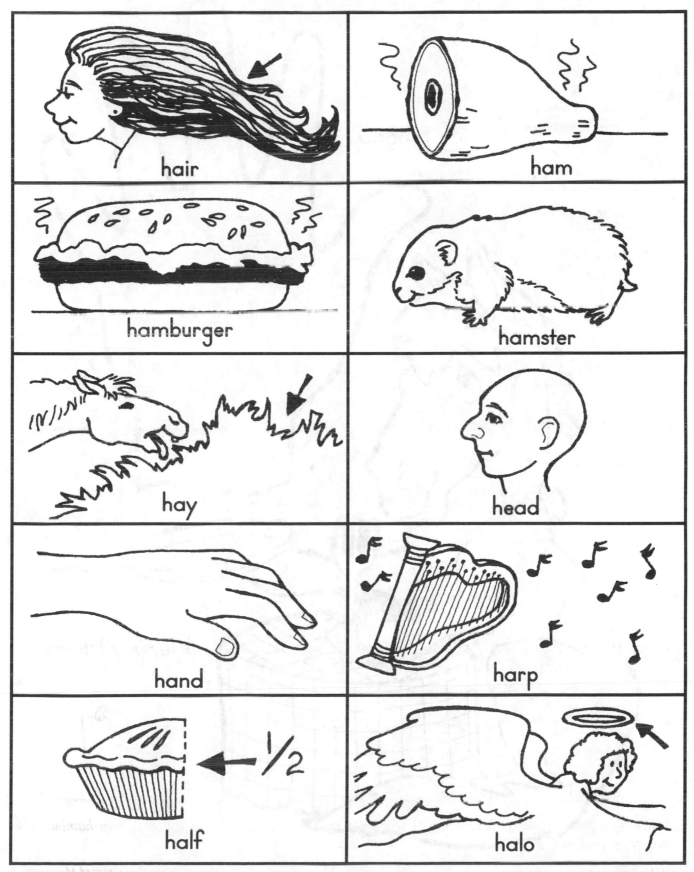

hair

ham

hamburger

hamster

hay

head

hand

harp

half

halo

Introducing the Letter H h (cont.)

Patterns

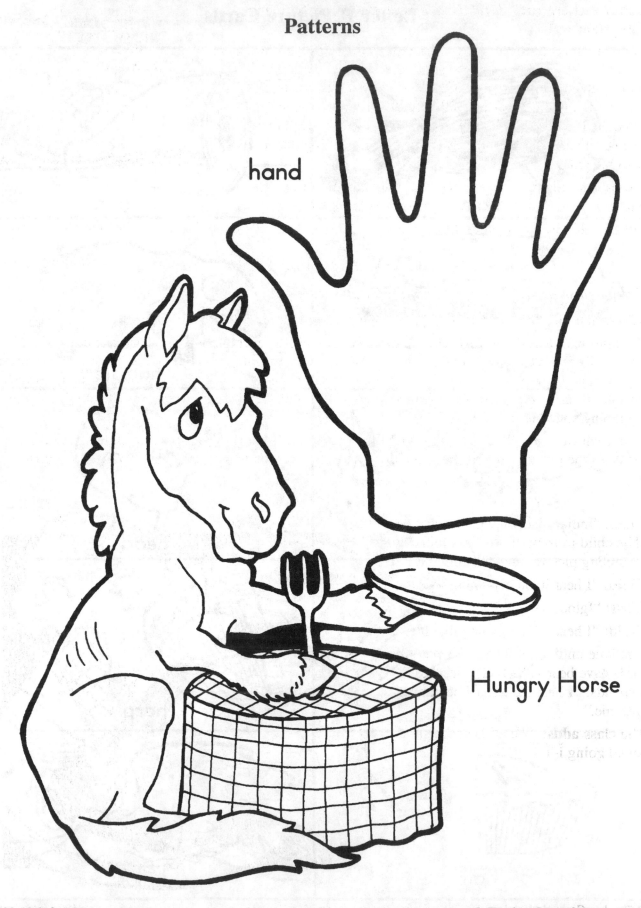

hand

Hungry Horse

74

Introducing the Letter I i

Letter I Literature: *If You Give a Mouse a Cookie* by Laura Joffe Numeroff

Look at the cover of the book. Have the children find all of the I's in the title. After reading, list all of the things that the mouse asked for, wanted, or did in the story. Give children pieces of drawing paper and tell them that they are going to illustrate their own "If You Give a..." stories, but instead of giving a mouse a cookie they have to give something that starts with the letter I.

Examples: Short I—If you give an infant a bottle of ink, he will illustrate. (iguana, insect, inchworm, igloo, invitation, etc.)

Long I—If you give an island ice, you can ice-skate. (Ira, iris, icing, ice cream, ivy, etc.)

What Do You Hear?

(Long and short sounds may be presented separately.)

Materials: long and short letter I picture cards (reproduced, colored, and laminated)

Working with one set of cards at a time, show the children each picture cards and ask them to name the object. Repeat the word, emphasizing the I sound, for example, ĭ–ĭ–ĭ–ink. Talk about the two different sounds that the letter I makes. Tell the children that when they sound out the long I sound, it says its own name, as when they say the alphabet: *H, I, J.* When they sound out the short I sound, it is the beginning sound in inch and if.

Give each card to a child. Pick one child to come up in front of the class. That child shows the rest of the class the picture card he/she is holding. The class responds with the chant "What Do You Hear?"

Short I

Class: "Indian, Indian, what do you hear?" (The child in front of the class looks at the remaining pictures and calls on one.)

Child: "I hear igloo beginning like me."

Class: "Igloo, igloo, what do you hear?"

Child: "I hear ink beginning like me."

Continue until all of the short I picture cards have been called. The last child responds: "I hear the letter I beginning with me."

The class adds: "We all hear the short sound going ĭ–ĭ–ĭ–ĭ!"

Introducing the Letter I i *(cont.)*

What Do You Hear? *(cont.)*

Long I

Class: "Ivy, ivy, what do you hear?"

Child: "I hear iron beginning like me."

Class: "Iron, iron, what do you hear?"

Child: "I hear ice beginning like me."

Continue until all of the long **I** picture cards have been called. The last child responds: "I hear the letter **I** beginning with me."

The class adds: "We all hear the long **I** sound going ī–ī–ī–ī

I is an Interesting Letter

Materials: several large pieces of construction paper or poster board with a large capital and lowercase **i** written on each, glue, crayons, I items (invitations, colored icing, plastic icicles, ink blots made by pouring a small amount of ink on paper)

Divide the class into groups of four or five. The children work together to glue the **I** items over the **I i**. When the glue dries, display the pictures on a bulletin board or wall.

Bulletin Board

Materials: crayons, markers, paper, scissors, copies of picture cards or other short and long **I** worksheets, glue, copies of the icicle and igloo patterns for each child

Make one large copy of the icicle and write the following directions on it: *Please help decorate an icicle with pictures that begin with the long I sound.*

Make one large copy of the igloo and write the following directions on it: *Please help decorate an igloo with pictures that begin with the short I sound.*

Staple the icicle and igloo to the bulletin board. Show the bulletin board to the children and explain the directions to them.

Have the children cut out their icicles and igloos and decorate the icicles with long **I** pictures and the igloos with short **I** pictures, using pictures they have drawn, or cut from magazines, or worksheets they have colored. Staple their finished icicles and igloos on the bulletin board.

Introducing the Letter I i *(cont.)*

Sounds and Pictures

Materials: the infant, Ina, and ice skates patterns (reproduced, colored, and laminated), invitation written on a large piece of poster board, short and long **I** picture cards, Velcro, hole punch, picture board, sound muncher

Punch a hole at the top of each long and short **I** picture card and hot glue a piece of Velcro to the back. Hot glue the matching piece of Velcro to the ice skates or the invitation.

Mix the long and short **I** pictures up and hang them on the picture board.

Hang the ice skates and invitation on the wall where the children can see and touch them. Place Ina by the ice skates and the infant by the invitation.

Gather the children by Ina, the ice skates, infant, invitation, and the picture board.

Short I

Tell the children: "I would like you to meet Inviting Infant. Inviting Infant enjoys inviting all of the iguanas and insects to his house for any occasion that comes along. He is always filling out invitations to mail to his iguana and insect friends. Inviting Infant makes a special ĭ–ĭ–ĭ–ĭ sound whenever he writes an invitation to one of this friends. (Have the children pretend to fill out an invitation while making the short sound like Inviting Infant does.) Inviting has brought a very special invitation with him today because he needs our help. He wants this special invitation to be decorated with interesting pictures that begin with the short **I** sound. Can you help him decorate his invitation with pictures that start with the same sound as infant, invitation, and the sound he makes, ĭ–ĭ–ĭ–ĭ?"

As you point to each picture on the board, the children name the object. Repeat the word, emphasizing the beginning sound of each word. Call the children one at a time to come up to the picture board and pick out a card. If the picture begins with a short **I** sound, he/she sticks it on the invitation. Inviting Indian and the children make the short **I** sound each time a new short **I** picture is added to the invitation.

Introducing the Letter I i *(cont.)*

Sounds and Pictures *(cont.)*

Long I

Tell the children: "Ice skater Ina is another visitor today. Ice skater Ina loves to skate on ice. She makes a special ī–ī –ī –ī sound as she skates around the rink. (Have the children pretend to ice skate while making the long ī–ī –ī –ī sound like Ina.) "Ice skater Ina has brought her ice skates with her today because she needs our help. She wants her ice skates to be decorated with pictures that begin with the long **I** sound. Can you help Ina decorate her ice skates with pictures that start with the same sound as Ina, ice skates, and the special sound she makes, ī–ī –ī –ī?"

As you point to each picture on the board, the children name the object. Repeat the word, emphasizing the beginning sound of each word. Call the children one at a time to come up to the picture board and pick out a card. If it begins with a long **I**, the child sticks it on the ice skates while Ina and the children make the long **I** sound.

Leave the ice skates, Ina, the invitation and Indian out in the classroom.

After you have done this activity a few times, mix up the pictures on the ice skates and the invitation.

Tell the children: "Ina skated by Inviting Indian's invitation last night and accidentally knocked all the pictures off of it and off of her ice skates. The pictures got all mixed up together, so she tried to stick them back up in the proper places, but she is not sure if she did it correctly."

Ask the children to look at the ice skates and invitation and identify any pictures which need to be moved from the ice skates to the invitation or vice versa.

If you want to challenge your class even more, add some non–**I** picture cards to both the ice skates and the invitation. Tell the students that the **I** pictures were mixed up with other picture cards. When they find a non–**I** picture card on the ice skates or invitation, have them feed it to the sound muncher. The children make the beginning sound of the non–**I** picture as the sound muncher eats it.

Introducing the Letter I i (cont.)

Sounds and Objects

Long I

Materials: island (large piece of poster board cut into the shape of an island), objects that begin with the long **I** sound (ice cube trays, ice cream containers, ice skates, icing, iris, iron, ivory, ivy)

Short I

Materials: invitation (large piece of construction paper with an invitation to something written on it), objects that begin with the short **I** sound (ink, insect, inch, infant-baby doll, Indian, instrument)

Place the island and invitation on the floor. Place all of the long and short **I** objects randomly on the island and invitation. Have the children name each object as you show it to the class. Repeat the word, emphasizing the beginning sound. As the objects are introduced to the class, place them on a table.

Each child comes up to the table and selects an object. If it begins like invitation, he/she places it on the invitation. If it begins like island, the child places it on the island.

When you feel that the children can distinguish between the long and short **I** sounds, you might like to challenge them by adding objects that begin with other sounds. If a child picks up one of these objects, he/she can feed it to the sound muncher. Have the child or the class make the beginning sound of the non–**I** object that is being eaten.

Letter Centers

Igloo

Materials: pieces of cardboard, sugar cubes, glue

Children glue sugar cubes to form an igloo on a piece of cardboard

Ink

Materials: paper, different colors of ink pens

Children write and draw pictures with various colors of ink pens.

I i Play Dough

Materials: play dough, cookie cutters in shapes that begin with the long and short **I** sound (Indian, insect, island, etc.)

Children press cookie cutters into the play dough to make pictures and patterns. They can also roll out the dough to form the capital and lowercase letters **I i**.

Insects

Materials: coloring pages that have pictures of insects, crayons

Children color in pictures of different insects.

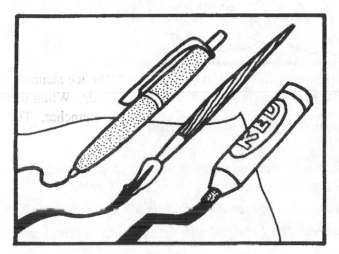

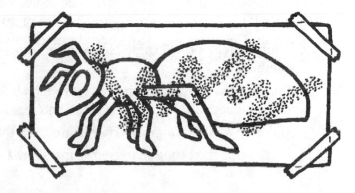

Introducing the Letter I i *(cont.)*

Let's Learn

• Before they respond to each question or direction that you give them, ask the children to identify which word or words begin with an **I**. Write the **I** words on a wall chart or on the chalkboard.

Let's Talk

• Name a type of musical instrument. (guitar, violin, flute)
• Name something that you would like to improve on in school. (reading, spelling, math)
• Name something that you might have to do when you are ill. (stay in bed, take medicine, go to the doctor)

Let's Move

• Move around the room like an inchworm and an iguana.
• Walk around the room like an Indian.
• Move around the room like you are on ice skates.

Let's Pretend

Pretend to:

• ice a cake
• build an igloo
• hold an infant

• get ice from an ice cube tray
• scoop ice cream into an ice cream cone

Let's Do

• Count "inchworms" (pipe cleaners cut into one-inch lengths) to correspond with oral or written numbers.
• Take a class ice cream survey. Have the children pick out their favorite flavor of ice cream: vanilla, chocolate, strawberry, etc., and record their responses on an "Ice Cream Graph."
• Make up a class tongue twister using long **I** words: *Ina ate ice cream while ice skating in Idaho.*
• Make up a class tongue twister using short **I** words: *The Indians invited an iguana, infant, and insect to Indiana.*

Introducing the Letter I i (cont.)

Long I Picture Cards   **Short I Picture Cards**

ivy

iguana

icicle

insect

ice

ink

ice cream

infant

iron

igloo

Introducing the Letter I i (cont.)

Patterns

Ice
Skater
Ina

icicle

igloo

82

Introducing the Letter I i *(cont.)*

Patterns *(cont.)*

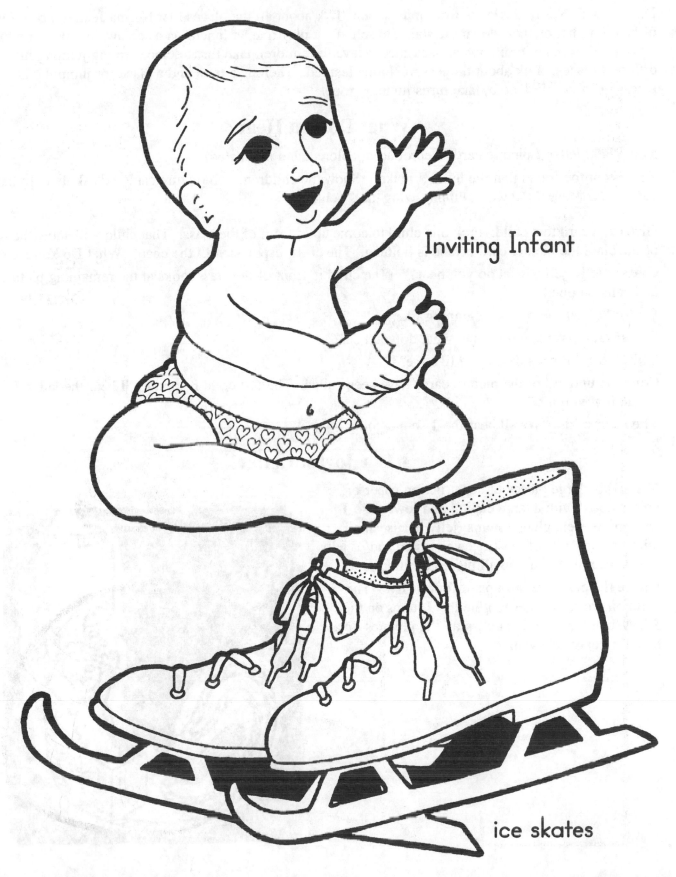

Inviting Infant

ice skates

Introducing the Letter J j

Letter J Literature: *Norma Jean, Jumping Bean* by Joanna Cole

Discuss why Norma's friends were mad at her. Talk about all the places that Norma Jean jumped: out of bed, into her clothes, down the stairs, to school, at playtime, at lunch, on a seesaw, in a pool, on the field, hurdles, high jump, potato-sack race. Have the children take turns demonstrating jumpng in different places. Talk about the lesson Norma learned. There is a time and a place for jumping; at recess or in the classroom, take turns jumping rope.

What Do You Hear?

Materials: letter **J** picture cards (reproduced, colored, and laminated)

Talk about the sound that the letter **J** makes. Show the children each picture card and ask them to name the object. Repeat the word, emphasizing the **J** sound

Give each card to a child. Pick one child to come up in front of the class. That child will show the rest of the class the picture card he/she is holding. The class responds with the chant "What Do You Hear?"

Class: "Jelly, jelly, what do you hear?" (The child in front of the class looks at the remaining pictures and calls on one.)

Child: "I hear jump rope beginning like me."

Class: "Jump rope, jump rope, what do you hear?"

Child: "I hear jeans beginning like me."

Continue until all of the picture cards have been called. The last child responds: "I hear the letter **J** beginning with me."

The class adds: "We all hear the **J** sound going j–j–j–j!"

J Is a Joyful Letter!

Materials: large pieces of construction paper or poster board with a large capital and lowercase **J** written on each, glue, **J** items (jelly beans, small juice cartons, bits of plastic jewelry, jam and/or jelly labels, jean materials, small pieces of jump rope)

Divide the class into groups of four or five. The children work together to glue the **J** items on the **J j**. When the glue dries, display the pictures on a bulletin board or a wall.

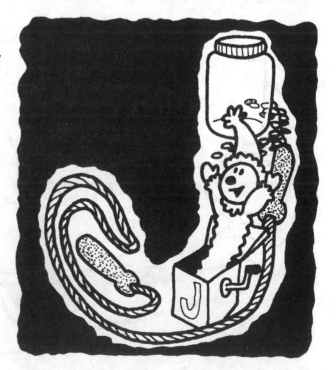

Introducing the Letter J j *(cont.)*

Bulletin Board

Materials: crayons or markers, paper, scissors, copies of picture cards or other **J** worksheets, glue, yarn, hole punch, copies of the jellyfish pattern for each child

Cut yarn into pieces to resemble the tentacles on the jellyfish.

Make one large copy of the jellyfish. Punch holes at the bottom of the jellyfish, string yarn through the holes, and knot. Write the following directions on the jellyfish: *Please help decorate a jolly jellyfish with pictures that begin with the letter* **J**.

Staple the jellyfish in the center of the bulletin board. Show the bulletin board to the children and explain the directions to them.

Give each child a copy of the jellyfish and several pieces of yarn. Have the children cut out their jellyfish and add tentacles. Ask the children to decorate their jellyfish with pictures that begin with the letter **J**, using pictures they have drawn, pictures cut from magazines, or worksheets they have colored. Staple their finished jellyfish onto the bulletin board.

The children can search at home for additional **J** pictures to be added to the bulletin board.

Sounds and Pictures

Materials: the juggler pattern (reproduced, colored, and laminated), a pair of jeans, **J** picture cards, some non–**J** picture cards, Velcro, hole punch, picture board, sound muncher

Punch a hole near the top of each picture card and hot glue a Velcro piece to the back. Hot glue the matching Velcro pieces to the jeans.

Place most of the **J** picture cards and some non-J picture cards on the picture board. Save a few **J** picture cards and several non–**J** picture cards to be added later.

Hang the pair of jeans on the wall where the children can see and touch them. Place the juggler by the pair of jeans.

Gather the children by the jeans, juggler, picture board, and sound muncher.

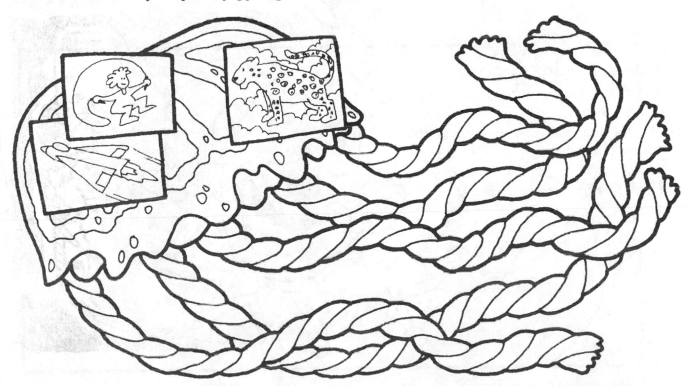

Introducing the Letter J j *(cont.)*

Sounds and Pictures *(cont.)*

Tell the children: "I would like you to meet Jolly Juggler. Jolly Juggler makes a special j–j–j–j sound whenever he juggles his jars of jelly. (Have the children pretend to juggle jars of jelly while making the j–j–j–j sound.) He has brought his jeans with him today because he needs our help. He wants us to help him decorate his jeans with pictures that begin with the letter **J**. Can you help decorate his jeans with pictures that start with the same sound as Jolly Juggler, jeans and the special sound that he makes when he juggles, j–j–j–j?"

As you point to each picture on the board, the children name the object. Repeat the word, emphasizing the beginning sound of each picture card. Call the children one at a time to come up to the picture board and pick out a card. If it begins with a **J**, the child sticks it on the jeans while Jolly Juggler and the children make the special j–j–j–j sound. If it does not begin with a **J**, he/she feeds it to the sound muncher. The child or the class makes the appropriate beginning sound while the picture is being eaten.

Leave the jeans and Jolly Juggler out in the classroom. After you have done this activity several times, mix up the pictures on the jeans and add some more **J** pictures and several non–**J** pictures to the pair of jeans.

Tell the children: "Jolly Juggler added some more pictures to his jeans, but he is not sure if they all begin with the **J** sound."

Point to each picture on the jeans and have the class say the word with you. Ask the children to look at the jeans and identify any pictures which need to be removed and fed to the sound muncher. Have the sound muncher and the children make the sound of the non–**J** picture as it is being eaten.

Introducing the Letter J j *(cont.)*

Sounds and Objects

Materials: long jump rope, objects that begin with the letter **J** (jar of jelly, jar of jam, jelly beans, jewelry, jeans, journal, toy jeep, jacks, jug, juice, jacket, jawbreakers), a few objects that begin with other sounds

Place the jump rope in the shape of a **J** on the floor. Place all of the **J** and non–**J** objects by the jump rope. Have the children name each object as you show it to the class. Repeat the word, emphasizing the beginning sound. As objects are named, place them on a table. Each child comes up to the table, selects an object, and says its name. If it begins like jump rope, the child places it by the jump rope. If it does not begin like jump rope, he/she feeds it to the sound muncher. As non–**J** objects are eaten, the child or the class makes its beginning sound.

Leave the jump rope and all of the **J** objects out as a display in the classroom.

Letter Centers

J j Play Dough

Materials: play dough, cookie cutters in shapes that begin with the letter **J** (jar, jug, jacket, etc.)

Children press the cookie cutters into the play dough to make patterns and pictures. They can also roll out the dough to form the capital and lowercase letters **J j**.

Jungle

Materials: jungle coloring book, crayons

Children color pictures of jungle scenes and animals.

Jeep Tracks

Materials: small toy jeeps, shallow pans of paint, paper

Children drive their jeeps through the paint and then make jeep tracks all over their papers.

Let's Learn

Before they respond to each question or direction that you give them, ask the children to identify which word or words begin with a **J**. Write the **J** words on a wall chart or on the chalkboard.

Introducing the Letter J j *(cont.)*

Let's Learn *(cont.)*

Let's Talk

- Name a type of job. (teacher, lawyer, cook, sales clerk)
- Name a month that starts with the letter J (January, June, July)
- Name a flavor of jelly. (grape, strawberry, blackberry)
- Name something you might see in a jungle. (monkeys, elephant, giraffe)
- Have you ever been jealous of someone? Tell how you handled your feelings.
- Name a type of juice that you like to drink. (orange, apple, grape)
- Where is your jaw?
- Name a part of a jacket. (pockets, collar, sleeve)
- Name a type of jewelry. (ring, bracelet, watch, necklace)

Let's Move

- Move around the room like a jaguar and jackal.
- Do several jumping jacks.
- Jog in place.

Let's Pretend

Pretend to:
- juggle
- drive a jeep through a jungle
- jump a jump rope
- be a jockey on a horse in a race
- be a jack-in-the-box
- put on your jacket

Let's Do

- Count out jelly beans to correspond with oral or written numbers.
- Open a bag of jellybeans, let the children sort them according to flavor. Count and record how many of each flavor were in the bag and graph the result on a "Jellybean Graph."
- Make up a class tongue twister using **J** words: *In June and July Jolly Jake juggles jelly beans and jam jars.*

88   © *Teacher Created Materials, Inc.*

Introducing the Letter J j *(cont.)*

Letter J Picture Cards

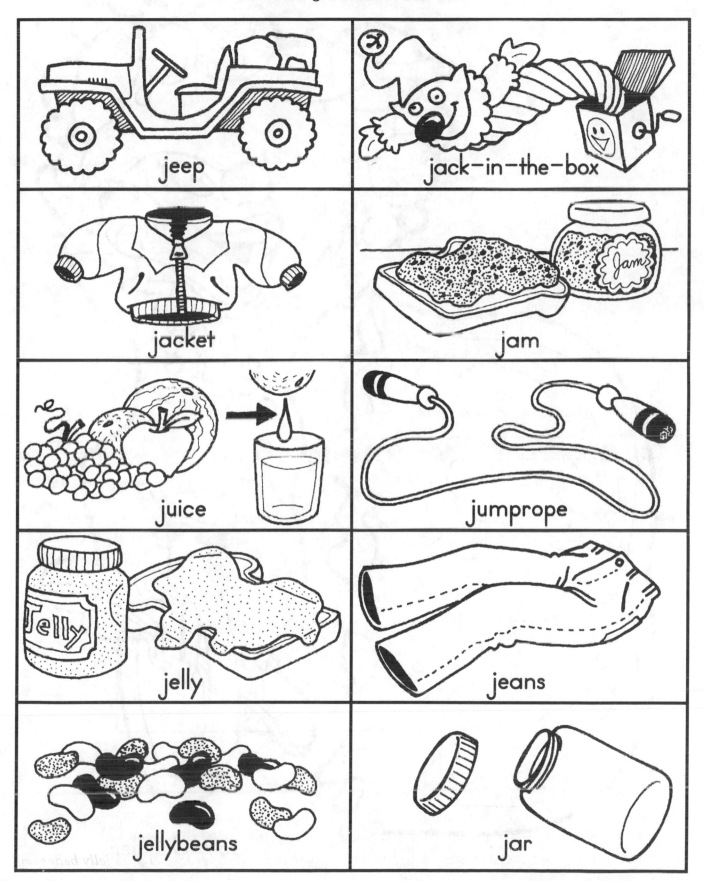

jeep

jack-in-the-box

jacket

jam

juice

jumprope

jelly

jeans

jellybeans

jar

Introducing the Letter J j *(cont.)*

Patterns

jellyfish

Jolly Juggler

Introducing the Letter K k

Letter K Literature: *Curious George Flies a Kite* by Margaret and H.A. Rey

Materials: construction paper, crayons, markers

Curious George found several uses for a piece of string. Ask the children to think of other ways to use string. Have they ever made a kite? What materials do they need for a kite? Have they flown a kite? Did the kite get caught in a tree? How did they get it down?

Have each child design his/her own kite on a piece of construction paper.

What Do You Hear?

Materials: letter **K** picture cards (reproduced, colored, and laminated)

Talk about the sound that the letter **K** makes. Show the children each picture card and ask them to name the object. Repeat the word, emphasizing the **K** sound.

Give each card to a child. Pick one child to come up in front of the class. That child shows the rest of the class the picture card he/she is holding. The class responds with the chant "What Do You Hear?"

Class: "Kangaroo, kangaroo, what do you hear?" (The child in the front of the class looks at the remaining pictures and calls on one.)

Child: "I hear key beginning like me."

Class: "Key, key, what do you hear?"

Child: "I hear kite beginning like me."

Continue until all of the picture cards have been called. The last child responds: "I hear the letter **K** beginning with me."

The class adds: "We all hear the sound **K** going k–k–k–k!"

K Is a Kind Letter!

Materials: large pieces of construction paper or poster board with a large capital and lowercase **K** printed on each, glue, **K** items (keys, popcorn kernels, empty ketchup packets, kidney beans)

Divide the class into groups of four or five. The children work together to glue the **K** items on the **K k**. When the glue dries, display the pictures on a bulletin board or a wall.

Introducing the Letter K k *(cont.)*

Bulletin Board

Materials: crayons, markers, paper, scissors, copies of picture cards or other **K** worksheets, glue, copies of the key pattern for each child

Make one large copy of the key. Write the following directions on it: *Please help decorate a kitchen key with pictures that begin with the letter **K**.*

Staple the key in the center of the bulletin board. Show the bulletin board to the children and explain the directions to them.

Give each child a copy of the key to cut out and color. Ask them to decorate their keys with pictures that begin with the letter **K**, using pictures that they have drawn, pictures cut from magazines, or worksheets that they have colored. Staple their finished keys onto the bulletin board.

The children can search at home for additional pictures that begin with the letter **K** to be added to the bulletin board.

Sounds and Pictures

Materials: kangaroo (use a stuffed one or a reproduced, colored, and laminated kangaroo pattern), kettle cut from black paper and laminated, **K** picture cards, some non–**K** picture cards, Velcro, hole punch, picture board, sound muncher

Punch a hole near the top of each picture card and hot glue a Velcro piece to the back. Hot glue the matching Velcro piece to the kettle.

Place most of the **K** picture cards and some non–**K** picture cards on the picture board. Save a few **K** picture cards and several non–**K** picture cards to be added later.

Hang the kettle on the wall where the children can see and touch it. Place the kangaroo beside the kettle.

Gather the children by the kettle, kangaroo, picture board, and sound muncher.

Introducing the Letter K k *(cont.)*

Sounds and Pictures *(cont.)*

Tell the children: "I would like you to meet Kooky Kangaroo. Kooky Kangaroo is different from other kangaroos because when she is in her kitchen making kidney beans in her kettle she makes a special k–k–k–k sound when she mixes up her ingredients. (Have the children pretend to hold spoons in their hands and mix the ingredients while saying k–k–k–k.) She has brought her kettle of kidney beans with her today because she needs our help. She thinks that her kidney beans will taste better if her kettle is decorated with pictures that start with the letter **K**. Can you help decorate her kettle with pictures that start with the same sound as kangaroo, kettle, and the special k–k–k–k sound she makes when she mixes her kidney beans?"

As you point to each picture on the board, the children name the object. Repeat the word, emphasizing the beginning sound of each picture card. Call the children one at a time to come up to the picture board and pick out a card. If it begins with a **K**, the child sticks it on the kettle while Kooky Kangaroo and the children make the k–k–k–k sound. If the picture on the card does not begin with a **K**, he/she feeds it to the sound muncher. The child or the class makes the beginning sound of the non–**K** picture that is being eaten.

Leave the kettle and Kooky Kangaroo out in the classroom. After you have done this activity several times, add more **K** pictures and several non–**K** pictures to the kettle.

Tell the children: "Kooky Kangaroo added some more pictures to her kettle, but she is not sure if they all begin with the letter **K**."

Point to each picture on the kettle and have the class say the word with you. Ask the children to look at the kettle and identify any pictures which need to be fed to the sound muncher. Have the sound muncher and the children make the sound of the non–**K** picture as it is being eaten.

Sounds and Objects

Materials: kite with a long tail, objects that begin with the letter **K** (keys, kaleidoscope, a bag of popcorn kernels, ketchup, can and/or bag of kidney beans, kilt, first aid kit, play doctor kit, toy kitten, toy koala), several objects that begin with other sounds

Introducing the Letter K k *(cont.)*

Sounds and Objects *(cont.)*

Place the kite on the floor. Place all of the **K** objects and non–**K** objects on and by the kite. Have the children name each object as you show it to the class. Repeat the word, emphasizing the beginning sound. As objects are named, place them on a table.

Each child comes up to the table, selects an object, and says its name. If it begins like kite, the child places it on or by the kite. If it does not begin like kite, he/she feeds it to the sound muncher. The child or the class makes the beginning sound of the non–**K** object as it is being eaten.

Leave the kite and all of the **K** objects out as a display in the classroom.

Letter Centers

Kitchen

Materials: play kitchen utensils, dishes, empty food containers and boxes, play food

Children play, mix and create food items in their kitchen.

Key Chain Rubbings

Materials: engraved metal key chains, paper, crayons

Children place paper on top of key chains and rub with a crayon.

Stamp Pad

Materials: keys hot glued to a small piece of wood, paper and several differently colored stamp pads

Children press keys on stamp pads and then on paper to make a beautiful key picture. Encourage the children to use different colors of ink and to overlap the keys.

K k Play Dough

Materials: play dough, keys, cookie cutters in shapes of objects that begin with the letter **K** (kitten, kite, key, kangaroo, etc.)

Children press keys and cookie cutters into the play dough to form pictures and patterns. They can also roll the play dough to form the capital and lowercase letters **K k**.

Let's Learn

Before they respond to each question or direction that you give them, ask the children to identify which word or words begin with a **K**. Write the **K** words on a wall chart or on the chalkboard.

Introducing the Letter K k *(cont.)*

Let's Talk

- Name something that you put ketchup on. (French fries, hamburger, hot dog)
- Name something that you keep in a special place. (diary, toys, jewelry)
- Name something that you might need a key to unlock. (car, door, locker, diary, safe)
- Name something that you would find in a first aid kit. (bandage, medicine, antiseptic cream)
- Name something that you would find in a doctor's kit. (needles, medicine, tongue depressor)
- Name something that you would find in a kitchen. (stove, microwave, refrigerator)
- Name something that a kitten needs. (water, love, food)

Let's Move

- Kick your foot forwards, backwards, and sideways.
- Move around the room like a kitten, a kangaroo, and a koala.
- Walk around the room like you are a king.

Let's Pretend

Pretend to:

- fly a kite
- look through a kaleidoscope
- put a key in a treasure chest and open it up
- play with a kitten
- play a kazoo

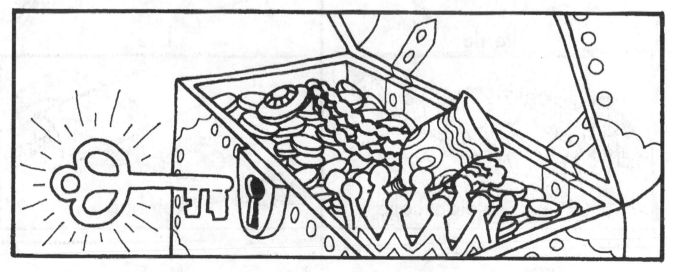

Let's Do

- Count out kidney beans to correspond with oral or written numbers.
- Make up a class tongue twister using **K** words: *King Kind keeps kittens, kangaroos, and koalas in his kitchen.*

Introducing the Letter K k *(cont.)*

Picture Cards

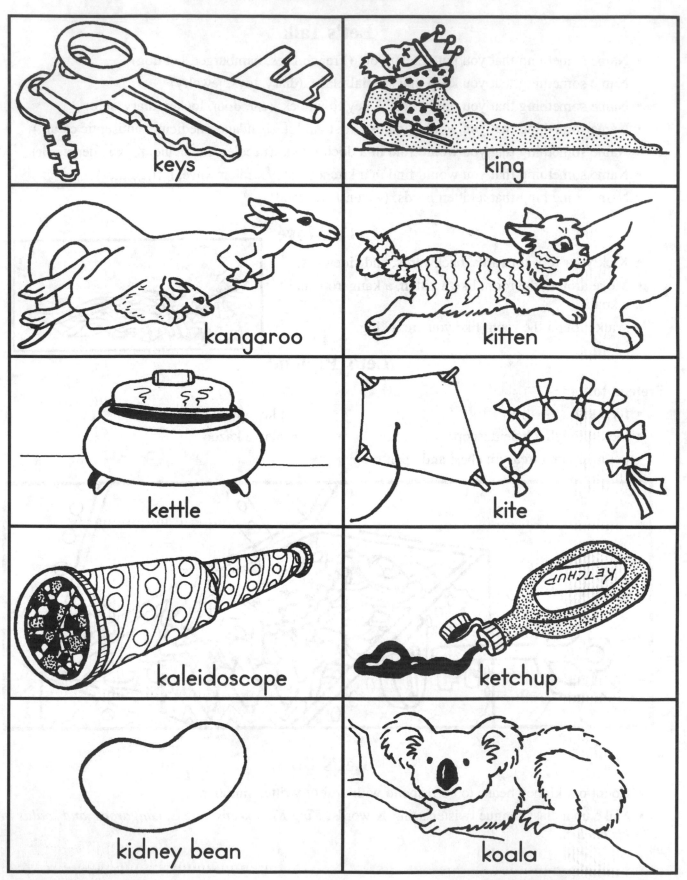

keys

king

kangaroo

kitten

kettle

kite

kaleidoscope

ketchup

kidney bean

koala

Introducing the Letter K k (cont.)

Patterns

key

kettle

Kooky Kangaroo

Introducing the Letter L l

Letter L Literature: *Lost* by David McPhail

After reading *Lost*, talk about all the places the boy and the bear went and the things they did while trying to find the bear's home. Let the children share experiences of being lost and what they did. Talk about what you should do if you are lost. Practice addresses and telephone numbers.

What Do You Hear?

Materials: letter **L** picture cards (reproduced, colored, and laminated)

Talk about the sound that the letter **L** makes. Show the children each of the picture cards and ask them to name the object. Repeat the word, emphasizing the **L** sound.

Give each card to a child. Pick one child to come up in front of the class. That child will show the rest of the class the picture card he/she is holding. The class responds with the chant "What Do You Hear?"

Class: "Lion, lion, what do you hear?" (The student in front of the class looks at the remaining pictures and calls on one.)

Child: "I hear lemon beginning like me."

Class: "Lemon, lemon, what do you hear?"

Child: "I hear lollipop beginning like me."

Continue until all of the picture cards have been called. The last child responds: "I hear the sound **L** beginning with me."

The class adds: "We all hear the **L** sound going l–l–l–l!"

L Is a Lovely Letter!

Materials: several large pieces of construction paper or poster board with a large capital and lowercase **L** printed on them, glue, **L** items (leaves, lids, lace, lollipop wrappers, lima beans, letters, lemon drops, licorice pieces, linoleum pieces)

Divide the class into groups of four or five. The children work together to glue the **L** items over the **L l**. When the pictures dry, display them on a bulletin board or a wall.

Introducing the Letter L l *(cont.)*

Bulletin Board

Materials: crayons, markers, paper, scissors, copies of picture cards or other **L** worksheets, glue, copies of the leaf pattern for each child

Make a large tree trunk and branches from brown construction paper and staple it to the bulletin board. Make one large copy of the leaf pattern and write the following directions on it: *Please help decorate a lovely leaf with pictures that begin with the letter **L**.* Staple the leaf to the tree.

Show the bulletin board to the children and explain the directions to them.

Give each child a copy of the leaf pattern to cut out and color. Children can decorate their leaves using pictures that they have drawn themselves, or pictures cut from magazines, or worksheets they have colored. Staple their finished leaves to the tree branches on the bulletin board.

The children can search at home for additional **L** pictures to be added to the bulletin board.

Sounds and Pictures

Materials: lion (use a stuffed one or a reproduced, colored, and laminated lion pattern), lace tablecloth or yard goods, paper clips, **L** picture cards, some non–**L** picture cards, hole punch, picture board, sound muncher

Punch a hole at the top of each picture card.

Place most of the **L** picture cards and some non–**L** picture cards on the picture board. Save a few **L** picture cards and several non–**L** picture cards to be added later.

Hang the lace on the wall where the children can see and touch it. Place the lion beside the lace. Bend paper clips and attach them to the lace to be used as hooks for the children to hang the picture cards.

Gather the children by the lace, lion, picture board, and sound muncher.

Tell the children: "I would like you to meet Lazy Lion. Lazy Lion is so lazy that instead of roaring loudly and furiously like most lions, she makes a lazy l–l–l–l sound. (Have the children make the l–l–l–l sound like Lazy Lion does.) She has brought her lace with her today because she needs our help. She was supposed to decorate this piece of lace for her friend the ladybug with pictures that start with the letter **L**. Can you help her decorate this piece of lace with pictures that start with the same sound as lion, lace, and the lazy sound she makes, l–l–l–l?"

Introducing the Letter L l *(cont.)*

Sounds and Pictures *(cont.)*

As you point to each picture on the picture board, ask the children to name the object. Repeat each word, emphasizing the beginning sound of each picture word. Call the children one at a time to come up to the picture board and pick out a card. If it begins with an **L**, the child hangs it on the lace while Lazy Lion and the children make the sound l–l–l–l. If the object does not begin with an **L**, he/she feeds it to the sound muncher. Have the child or the class make the beginning sound of the picture non–**L** picture as it is being eaten.

Leave the lace and Lazy Lion out in the classroom.

After you have done this activity several times, mix up the pictures on the lace and add some more **L** pictures and several non–**L** pictures to the lace.

Tell the children: "Lazy Lion added some more pictures to the lace, but she is not sure if they all begin with the letter **L**."

Point to each picture on the lace and have the class name the object with you. Ask them to tell you which pictures need to be fed to the sound muncher. Have the sound muncher and the children make the sound of the non–**L** picture as it is being eaten.

Sounds and Objects

Materials: stepladder, objects that begin with the letter **L** (lemon, lemonade container, lamp, leaf, lid, lock, light bulb, lima beans, lace, ladle, lunch box, piece of leather, lipstick, lollipop, lime, letter, small log, library card), a few objects that begin with other sounds

Place all of the **L** and non–**L** objects on or by the ladder. Have the children name each object as you show it to the class. Repeat the word, emphasizing the beginning sound. As objects are named, place them on a table.

Each child comes up to the table, selects an object, and says its name. If it begins like ladder, the child places it on the ladder. If it does not begin like ladder, he/she feeds it to the sound muncher. Have the child or the class make the sound of the non–**L** object as it is being eaten.

Leave the ladder and all of the **L** objects out as a display in the classroom.

Introducing the Letter L l *(cont.)*

Letter Centers

Lace Rubbings

Materials: pieces of lace in different sizes and textures, paper, crayons

Children lay paper on top of lace and rub with a crayon.

Library Cards

Materials: library books, a card with the name of each book written on it

Children match the library card to the correct book and slip the card into the pocket.

Lollipop Lids

Materials: large plastic lids from coffee cans or margarine tubs with holes punched around the edges, colorful yarn cut into long pieces with one end taped like the end of a shoe string, craft sticks, hot glue gun

Children weave the yarn in and out of the holes in the lids. The teacher hot glues a craft stick to the back of the lid to make a lollipop.

L l Play Dough

Materials: play dough, lids, cookie cutters in shapes of objects that begin with the letter L (leaf, lobster, lemon, etc.)

Children press lids and cookie cutters into the play dough to form pictures and patterns. They can also roll the dough to form the capital and lowercase **L l**.

Let's Learn

Before they respond to each question or direction that you give them, ask the children to identify which word or words begin with an **L**. Write the **L** words on a wall chart or on the chalkboard.

Introducing the Letter L l *(cont.)*

Let's Learn *(cont.)*

Let's Talk

- Name someone you love. (mother, father, sister, etc.)
- Name something that makes you laugh. (cartoons, friends, jokes)
- Name something that you would find on a license plate. (state, numbers, expiration date)
- Name something that you lick. (stamps, Popsicle, envelopes, ice-cream cone, lollipop, etc.)
- Name something that you would see in a library. (books, librarian, magazines)
- What does it mean to tell a lie? How do you feel after you have told a lie?
- Name something that you might find in a lunch box. (sandwich, drink, napkin)
- Name something that you would put a lock on. (trunk, door, locker)
- Name something that you have loaned to your brother, sister, or friend. (toy, book, money)
- Name something or someone who is little. (Thumbelina, ant, crumb)
- Name something that people eat for lunch. (sandwich, apple, soup)

Let's Move

- Lean left, right, forwards, and backwards.
- Leap to the left.
- Lift your left arm, left leg, and left hand.
- Move around the room like a leopard, lizard, llama, lobster, and a lion.

Let's Pretend

Pretend to:

- climb up and down a ladder
- hang up laundry on a laundry line
- start a lawnmower
- write a letter
- make and drink fresh-squeezed lemonade

Let's Do

- Count out lids to correspond with oral or written numbers.
- Open a bag of assorted lollipops. Let the children sort the lollipops according to flavor. Count and record how many of each flavor were in the bag and graph the results on a "Lollipop Graph."
- Sort a variety of lids according to size, colors, the foods they come from.
- Make up a class tongue twister using **L** words: *Lizzy Lizard likes lemon and lime lollipops.*

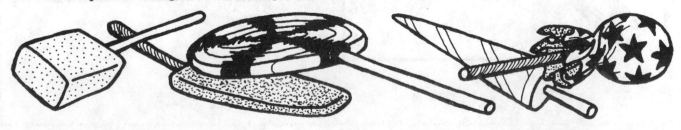

Introducing the Letter L l *(cont.)*

Letter L Picture Cards

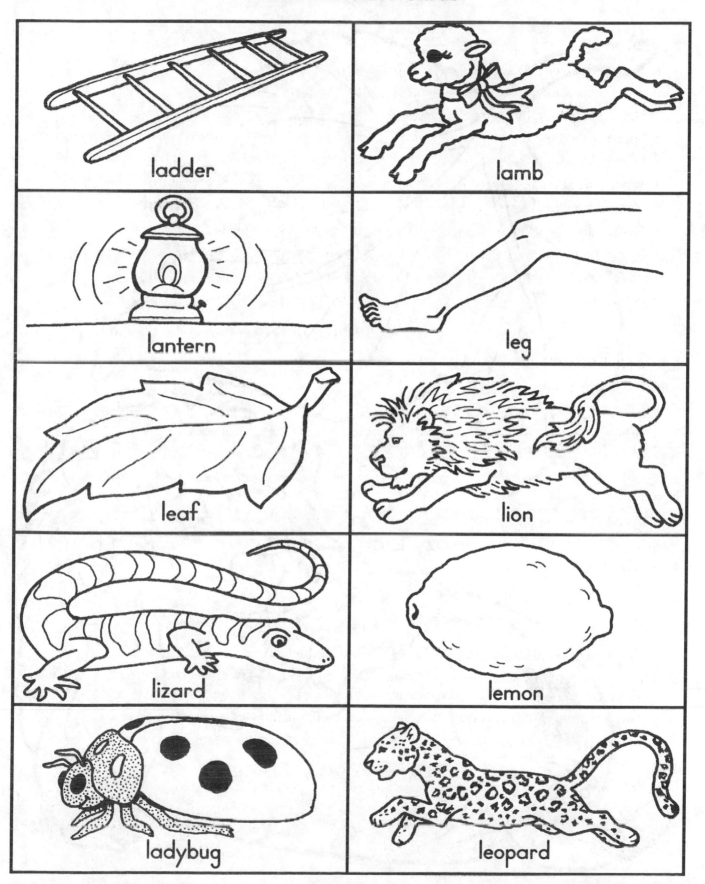

ladder

lamb

lantern

leg

leaf

lion

lizard

lemon

ladybug

leopard

Introducing the Letter L l (cont.)

Patterns

leaf

Lazy Lion

Introducing the Letter M m

Letter M Literature: *Happy Birthday Moon* by Frank Asch

Materials: wall chart, markers, yellow construction paper cut in a circle to resemble a full moon for each child, crayons

Before reading the book show the cover to the children. Ask them to point out the word and picture that begins with the letter **M**. Ask them to listen for words that begin with the **M** sound in the story and raise their hands each time they hear an **M** word. As each new **M** word is read, write it on the wall chart (moon, maybe, mountains, moment, money, morning).

Read *Happy Birthday Moon*. Talk about the characters and the different places the bear goes in the story. Ask the children why they think the moon repeats everything that the bear says. Discuss echoes. Ask the children what birthday present they would give the moon if they could. Try to think of presents the moon could use in the sky, such as a kite, yo-yo, airplane, sparklers, bubbles, balloons, etc.

Give each child a yellow moon. Tell them to draw a picture of a present that they would like to give the moon for his birthday.

What Do You Hear?

Materials: letter **M** picture cards
(reproduce, color, and laminate)

Talk about the sound that the letter **M** makes. Show the children each picture card and ask them to name the object. Repeat the word, emphasizing the **M** sound.

Give each card to a child. Pick one child to come up in front of the class. That child will show the rest of the class the picture card he/she is holding. The class responds with the chant "What Do You Hear?"

Class: "Mouse, mouse, what do you hear?" (The child in front of the class looks at the remaining pictures and picks one to call next.)

Child: "I hear mitten beginning like me."

Class: "Mitten, mitten, what do you hear?"

Child: "I hear marshmallow beginning like me."

Continue until all of the picture cards have been called. The last child responds: "I hear the letter **M** beginning with me."

The class adds: "We all hear the **M** sound going m–m–m–m!"

Introducing the Letter M m *(cont.)*

M Is a Magnificent Letter!

Materials: large pieces of construction paper or poster board with a large capital and lowercase **M** printed on each, glue, **M** items (macaroni noodles, mini marshmallows, M&M's wrappers, mail, cut up pieces from a map, cut up pieces from a place mat, margarine container, magazine covers, empty match books)

Divide the class into groups of four or five. The children work together to glue the **M** items on the **M m**. When the glue dries, display the pictures on a bulletin board or a wall.

Bulletin Board

Materials: crayons or markers, paper, scissors, copies of picture cards or other worksheets, glue **M**, copies of the mailbox pattern for each child, brads

Make one large copy of the mailbox. Write the following directions on the large mailbox:

Please help decorate a mailbox with marvelous pictures that begin with the letter M.

Staple the large mailbox in the center of the bulletin board. Show the bulletin board to the children and explain the directions to them.

The children color and cut out their mailboxes and flags. Use brads to attach the flags to the mailboxes. Ask the children to decorate their mailboxes with pictures that begin with the letter **M**, using pictures that they have drawn, pictures cut from magazines, or worksheets that they have colored. Staple their finished mailboxes to the bulletin board.

The children can search at home for additional pictures that begin with **M** to add to the bulletin board.

Sounds and Pictures

Materials: mouse (use a stuffed one or a reproduced, colored, and laminated mouse pattern), monster's mitten (cut a mitten shape from fabric or paper), **M** picture cards, some non–**M** picture cards, Velcro, picture board, sound muncher

Punch a hole at the top of each picture card and hot glue a piece of Velcro to the back. Hot glue the matching Velcro pieces to the mitten.

Place most of the **M** picture cards and some non–**M** picture cards on the picture board. Save a few **M** picture cards and several non–**M** picture cards to be added later.

Introducing the Letter M m *(cont.)*

Sounds and Pictures *(cont.)*

Hang the monster's mitten on the wall where the children can see and touch it. Place the mouse by the mitten. Gather the children by the mitten, mouse, picture board, and sound muncher.

Tell the children: "I would like you to meet Missy Mouse. Missy Mouse is special because she does not squeak like other mice. Instead of squeaking, Missy makes a m–m–m–m sound whenever she gets excited. (Have the children make the m–m–m–m sound like Missy Mouse.) She has brought a mitten that once belonged to a monster with her today. The monster gave her the mitten to use as a blanket to keep her warm in the winter. Missy likes the mitten, but she would like to add some decorations that start with the letter **M** to make it look more exciting. Can you help her decorate her mitten with pictures that start with the same sound as mouse, mitten, and the m–m–m–m sound Missy makes when she is excited?"

As you point to each picture on the board, the children name the object. Repeat the word, emphasizing the beginning sound of each picture card. Call the children one at a time to come up to the picture board and pick out a card. If it begins with an **M**, the child sticks it on the mitten while Missy Mouse and the children make the special m–m–m–m sound. If it does not begin with an **M**, he/she feeds it to the sound muncher. The child or the class makes the beginning sound of the non–**M** picture as it is being eaten.

Leave the mitten and Missy Mouse out in the classroom. After you have done this activity several times, mix up the pictures on the mitten and add some more M pictures and several non–**M** pictures to the mitten.

Tell the children: "Missy Mouse added some more pictures to her mitten, but she is not sure if they all begin with the **M** sound."

Point to each picture on the mitten and have the class say the word with you. Ask the children to look at the mitten and identify any pictures which need removed and fed to the sound muncher. Have the sound muncher and the children make the beginning sound of the non–**M** picture as it is being eaten.

Introducing the Letter M m *(cont.)*

Sounds and Objects

Materials: large map, objects that begin with **M** (marshmallows, mittens, macaroni, mop, mail, mayonnaise, mustard, magnets, milk carton, magazines, marbles, mask, muffins, mushrooms, microphone, markers, mirror), several objects that begin with other sounds

Place the map on the floor. Place all of the **M** objects and non–**M** objects on top of the map. Have the children name each object as you show it to the class. Repeat the word, emphasizing the beginning sound. As objects are named, place them on a table.

Each child comes up to the table, selects an object, and says its name. If it begins like map, the child places it on the map. If it does not begin like map, he/she feeds it to the sound muncher. As non–**M** objects are eaten, the child or the class makes its beginning sound.

Leave the map and all of the **M** objects out as a display in the classroom.

Letter Centers

Musical Macaroni Milk Cartons

Materials: thoroughly washed lunchroom milk cartons, macaroni, stapler, glue, decorations

Children fill milk cartons with macaroni, staple the top shut, glue decorations on the outside, and make music.

Mosaics

Materials: small pieces cut from colored foam meat trays or white ones colored with markers, glue, colored construction paper

Children glue pieces of foam trays close together on construction paper to create mosaics.

Macaroni Necklaces

Materials: macaroni, yarn pieces with tape wrapped around one end like a shoestring

Children string yarn through macaroni to make necklaces that they can wear.

Marshmallow Prints

Materials: mini marshmallows, regular sized marshmallows, paper, colored paints, paper

Children dip marshmallows in the paints and press them on the paper to create colorful pictures.

M m Play Dough

Materials: play dough, marbles, macaroni, cookie cutters in shapes that begin with the letter **M** (monkey, mouse, mask, etc.)

Children press **M** items into the play dough to form pictures and patterns. They can also roll the dough to form the capital and lowercase letters **M m**.

Magnets

Materials: magnets of various sizes and shapes

Children experiment with magnets.

Introducing the Letter M m (cont.)

Let's Learn

Before they respond to each question or direction that you give them, ask the children to identify which word or words begin with an **M**. Write the M words on a wall chart or on the chalkboard.

Let's Talk

- Name something that you put margarine in or on. (toast, potato, pancakes, roll)
- Name something that you could order at McDonald's. (hamburger, French fries, soda, salad)
- Name a type of machine. (computer, typewriter, lawn mower, car)
- Name a good manner to have. (saying thank you, please, and excuse me)
- Name a bad manner. (talking with food in your mouth, not cleaning up a mess)
- Name something that you can make all by yourself. (bed, sandwich, picture)
- Name a trick that you have seen a magician do. (card, bunny, feathers)
- Describe how a marshmallow feels and tastes. (sticky, gooey, gummy, sweet, sugary)
- Name something that costs a lot of money to buy. (car, house, boat)

Let's Move

- Move around the room like a monkey, a mare, and/or a manatee.
- Deliver the mail to your friends.
- March around the room like you are in the military.
- Fly around the room like a magpie.

Let's Pretend

Pretend to:

- pour a glass of milk
- get, open and read your mail
- move a heavy piece of furniture
- make and mix macaroni
- mash potatoes

- catch a mackerel
- brush a mare's mane
- play marbles
- give yourself a manicure
- milk a cow

Let's Do

- Count out mini marshmallows to correspond with oral or written numbers.
- Save white and chocolate milk cartons from lunch, wash thoroughly, and use them to take a survey of which kind the children prefer - white or chocolate. Instead of recording the results on a graph, pile the results into two different stacks.
- Each child selects a white or chocolate carton and places it on the proper stack. (Place the cartons sideways so they will not tip over as easily).
- Make up a tongue twister using **M** words: *Mean Monster made me mad on Monday.*

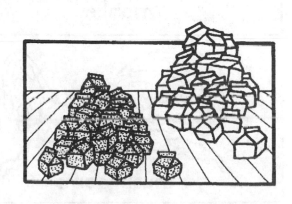

Introducing the Letter M m (cont.)

Letter M Picture Cards

map

moon

money

moose

mermaid

motorcycle

monkey

mountains

mushrooms

mouse

Introducing the Letter M m *(cont.)*

Letter M Picture Cards *(cont.)*

magnet

milk

mailbox

mirror

manatee

mittens

marble

medal

mask

mop

Introducing the Letter M m (cont.)

Patterns

Missy Mouse

Mitten

mailbox and flag

Introducing the Letter N n

Letter **N** Literature: *Arthur's Nose* by Marc Brown

Discuss why Arthur wants a new nose in the story (thought his looked funny, nuisance at school, was always found at hide-and-seek). List all of the noses that he tried on: chicken, fish, elephant, koala bear, hippopotamus, armadillo, toucan, goat, rabbit, mouse, zebra, alligator, and rhinoceros. Talk about what the last line in the story means.

What Do You Hear?

Materials: letter **N** picture cards (reproduce, color, and laminate)

Talk about the sound that the letter **N** makes. Show the children each picture card and ask them to name each object. Repeat the word, emphasizing the **N** sound.

Give each card to a child. Pick one child to come up in front of the class. That child shows the rest of the class the picture card he/she is holding. The class responds with the chant "What Do You Hear?"

Class: "Nail, nail, what do you hear?" (The child in front of the class looks at the remaining pictures and calls on one.)

Child: "I hear nickel beginning like me."

Class: "Nickel, nickel, what do you hear?"

Child: "I hear nest beginning like me."

Continue until all of the picture cards have been called. The last child responds: "I hear the letter **N** beginning like me."

The class adds: "We all hear the sound **N** going n–n–n–n!"

N Is a Nice Letter!

Materials: Several large pieces of construction paper or poster board, with a large capital and lowercase **N** printed on each, glue, **N** items (newspaper, noodles, name tags, pieces of net from fruit or vegetable bags, play money nickels, nails, numbers from a calendar)

Divide the class into groups of four or five. The children work together to glue the **N** items over the **N n**. When the glue dries, display the pictures on a bulletin board or wall.

Introducing the Letter N n *(cont.)*

Bulletin Board

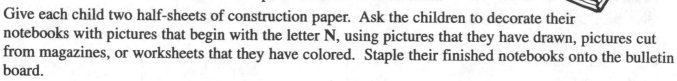

Materials: crayons, markers, scissors, glue, pictures of objects that begin the letter N, construction paper

Make a large notebook using two pieces of construction paper. Staple some of the children's letter N worksheets and handwriting paper between the construction paper covers. Write the following directions the notebook: *Please help decorate a nice notebook with pictures that begin with the letter N.*

Staple the large notebook to the center of the bulletin board. Show the bulletin board to the children and explain the directions to them.

Give each child two half-sheets of construction paper. Ask the children to decorate their notebooks with pictures that begin with the letter N, using pictures that they have drawn, pictures cut from magazines, or worksheets that they have colored. Staple their finished notebooks onto the bulletin board.

The children can search at home for additional pictures that begin with the letter N to add to the bulletin board.

Sounds and Pictures

Materials: reproduced, colored, and laminated the Neat Ned pattern, several neckties, N picture cards, some non–N picture cards, Velcro, hole punch, picture board, sound muncher

Punch a hole at the top of each picture card. Hot glue a piece of Velcro to the back of each picture card and hot glue the matching Velcro piece to the neckties.

Place most of the N picture cards and some non–N picture cards on the picture board. Save a few N picture cards and several non–N picture cards to be added later.

Hang the neckties on the wall where the children can see and touch them. Place the Neat Ned beside the neckties.

Gather the children by the neckties, Neat Ned, picture board, and sound muncher.

Tell the children: "I would like you to meet Neat Ned. Neat Ned loves to collect neckties. Every morning when he puts on his necktie he makes a noisy n–n–n–n sound. (Have the children pretend to put on a necktie and make the noise n–n–n–n sound like Ned.) He has brought some of his new neckties with him today because he needs our help. He thinks that he would look nifty if his neckties were decorated with pictures that start with the letter N. Can you help him decorate his neckties with pictures that start with the same sound as Ned, necktie, and the noisy sound that he makes, n–n–n–n?"

Introducing the Letter N n *(cont.)*

Sounds and Pictures *(cont.)*

As you point to each picture on the board, the children name the object. Repeat the word, emphasizing the beginning sound of each picture card. Call the children one at a time to come up to the picture board and pick out a card. If it begins with an **N**, the child sticks it on a necktie while Neat Ned and the children make the noisy sound n–n–n–n. If it does not begin with an **N**, he/she feeds it to the sound muncher. The child or the class makes the beginning sound of the non–**N** picture as it is being eaten.

Leave the neckties and Neat Ned out in the classroom. After you have done this activity several times, mix up the pictures on the neckties and add some more **N** pictures and several non–**N** pictures to the neckties.

Tell the children: "Neat Ned added some more pictures to his neckties, but he is not sure if they all begin with the **N** sound." Point to each picture on the necktie and have the class say the word with you. Ask them to identify any pictures which need to be removed and fed to the sound muncher. Have the sound muncher and the children make the beginning sound of the non–**N** picture as it is being eaten.

Sounds and Objects

Materials: newspaper, objects that begin with the letter **N** (nails, nail brush, nail polish, nectarine, noodles, nickels, necklace, nuts, nest, necktie, needles, nylon, needlepoint, name tag, net, note, nutmeg, name tags), a few objects that begin with other sounds

Spread the newspaper out on the floor. Place all of the **N** and non–**N** objects on the newspaper. Have the children name each object as you show it to the class. Repeat the word, emphasizing the beginning sound. As the objects are introduced to the class, place them on a table.

Introducing the Letter N n *(cont.)*

Sounds and Objects *(cont.)*

Each child comes up to the table, selects an object, and says its name. If it begins like newspaper, the child places it on the newspaper. If it does not begin like newspaper, he/she feeds it to the sound muncher. Have the child or the class make the sound of the non–N object as it is being eaten.

Leave the newspaper and all of the **N** objects out as a display in the classroom.

Letter Centers

Net and Nickel Prints

Materials: net cut from orange, onion, or potato bags and nickels hot glued to one side of small pieces of wood; different colored stamp pads; paper

Children press nets and nickels on stamp pads and then onto paper to make a net and nickel picture. Encourage the children to use different colors of ink and to overlap their prints.

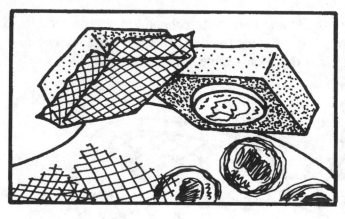

Numbers

Materials: numerals 0-9, cut from tag board, written on index cards, or plastic manipulatives

Children order numbers from lowest to highest, and/or group the odd and even numbers.

Newspaper

Materials: newspaper, Silly Putty

Children press Silly Putty down on the newspaper, look at the print on the silly putty, and then stretch the putty to make silly pictures.

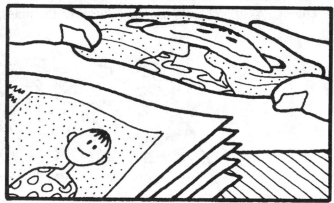

N n Play Dough

Materials: play dough, nickels, nuts, cookie cutters in shapes that begin with the letter **N** (nuts, nails, nurse, etc.)

Children press **N** items and cookie cutters into the play dough to make pictures and patterns. They can also roll the dough out to form the capital and lowercase letter **N n**.

Let's Learn

Before they respond to each question or direction that you give them, ask the children to identify which word or words begin with an **N**. Write the **N** words on a wall chart or on the chalkboard.

Introducing the Letter N n *(cont.)*

Let's Learn *(cont.)*

Let's Talk

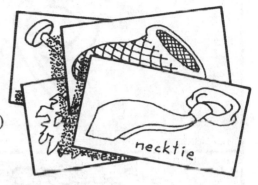

- Name a type of nut. (peanut, walnut, pecan)
- Name a time when you felt nervous. (first day of school, at the doctor's office, meeting someone new)
- Name some things that you would find in your neighborhood. (stores, post office, sidewalks)
- Name something that comes out at night. (stars, owls, bats)
- How can you tell if something is new? (shiny, clean, no marks)
- Do you have a nickname? What is it?
- Name something that is nutritious to eat. (apple, peas, oranges)

Let's Move

- Nod your head no and yes.
- Move around on the floor like a newt.

Let's Pretend

Pretend to:

- be a nurse and take someone's temperature and blood pressure and give a shot
- take a nap

Let's Do

- Count out nuts, nails, noodles, or nickels to correspond with oral or written numbers.
- Provide mixed nuts (in a shell). Have the children sort them by type, size, and/or color. Record on a "Nut Graph."
- Make up a tongue twister using **N** words: *Nancy's naughty niece never naps.*

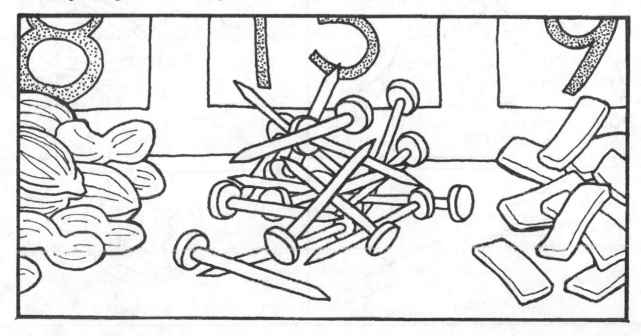

Introducing the Letter N n

Introducing the Letter N n (cont.)

Letter N Picture Cards

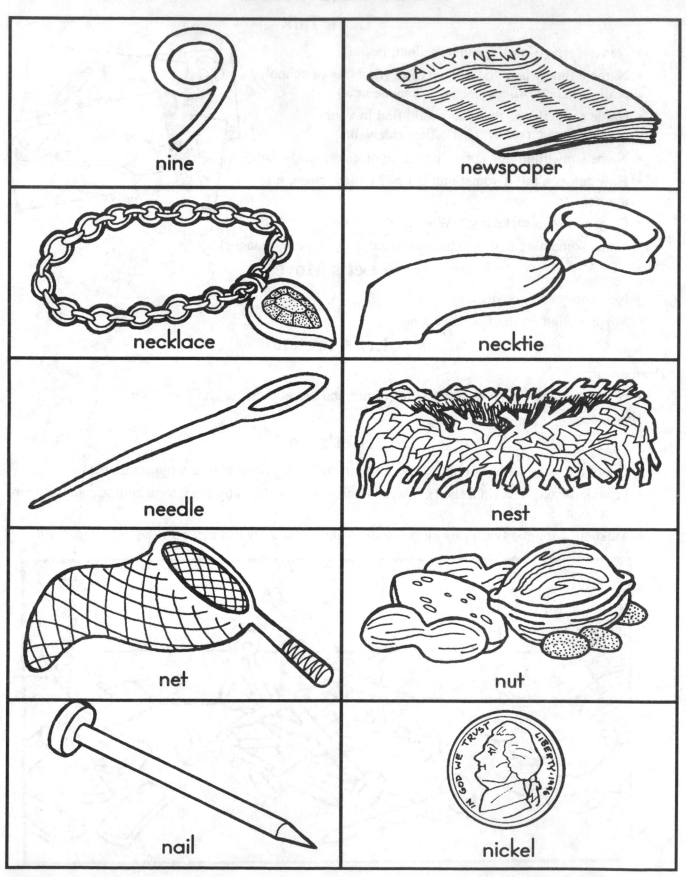

nine

newspaper

necklace

necktie

needle

nest

net

nut

nail

nickel

Introducing the Letter N n *(cont.)*

Patterns

Neat Ned

Necktie

Introducing the Letter O o

Letter O Literature: *Oscar Otter* by Nathaniel Benchley

Have the children find the two **O** words on the cover of the book. List all of the characters in the story. Ask the children how the beaver helped the otter. Discuss why the beaver was preparing his home for the winter. At recess time slide down a slide, pretending to be the otter, fox, wolf, mountain lion, and moose.

What Do You Hear?

(Long and short sounds may be presented separately.)

Materials: long and short letter **O** picture cards (reproduced, colored, and laminated)

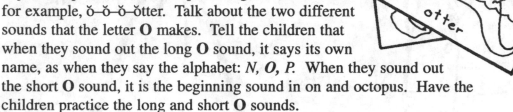

Working with one set of cards at a time, show the children each picture cards and ask them to name the object. Repeat the word, emphasizing the **O** sound, for example, ŏ–ŏ–ŏ–ŏtter. Talk about the two different sounds that the letter **O** makes. Tell the children that when they sound out the long **O** sound, it says its own name, as when they say the alphabet: *N, O, P.* When they sound out the short **O** sound, it is the beginning sound in on and octopus. Have the children practice the long and short **O** sounds.

Give each letter **O** card to a child. Pick one child to come up in front of the class. That child will show the rest of the class the picture card he/she is holding. The class responds with the chant "What Do You Hear?"

Short O

Class: "Octopus, octopus, what do you hear?" (The child in front of the class looks at the remaining pictures and calls on one.)

Child: "I hear olive beginning like me."

Class: "Olive, olive, what do you hear?"

Child: "I hear octagon beginning like me."

Continue until all of the short **O** picture cards have been called. The last child responds: "I hear the letter **O** beginning with me."

The class adds: "We all hear the short **O** sound going ŏ–ŏ–ŏ–ŏ!"

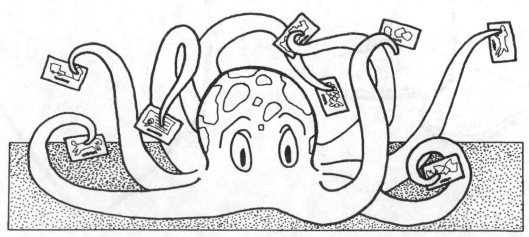

Introducing the Letter O o *(cont.)*

What Do You Hear? *(cont.)*

Long O

Class: "Ocean, ocean, what do you hear?" (The child in front of the class looks at the remaining pictures and calls on one.)

Child: "I hear oar beginning like me."

Class: "Oar, oar, what do you hear?"

Child: "I hear overalls beginning like me."

Continue until all of the long **O** picture cards have been called. The last child responds: "I hear the letter **O** beginning with me."

The class adds: "We all hear the long **O** sound going ō–ō–ō–ō!

O is an Outstanding Letter

Materials: several large pieces of construction paper or poster board, with a large capital and lowercase **O** written on each, glue, crayons, **O** items (oatmeal, overcoat, overshoes, can opener, octagons, O-shaped cereal, real or artificial oak leaves)

Divide the class into groups of four or five. The children work together to glue the **O** items over the **O o**. When the glue dries, display the pictures on a bulletin board or wall.

Bulletin Board

Materials: crayons, markers, paper, scissors, copies of picture cards or other worksheets, glue a long **O** and short **O**, copies of the octagon and oar patterns for each child

Make one large copy of the oar and write the following directions on it: *Please decorate an oar with pictures that begin with the long O sound.*

Make one large copy of the of the octagon and write the following directions on on it: *Please decorate an octagon with pictures that begin with the short O sound.*

Staple the oar and octagon to the bulletin board. Show the bulletin board to the children and explain the directions to them.

The children cut out and color their oars and octagons, and then decorate the oars with long **O** pictures and the octagons with short **O** pictures, using pictures they have drawn, or cut from magazines, or worksheets they have colored. Staple their finished oars and octagons on the bulletin board.

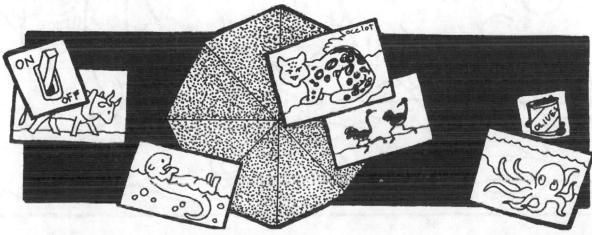

Introducing the Letter O o *(cont.)*

Sounds and Pictures

(For older or more advanced students, short and long sounds may be presented)

Materials: Reproduced, colored, and laminated opossum and octopus patterns, pair of overalls cut from blue construction paper or poster board, rectangular piece of bulletin board paper with an on-off switch drawn in the middle, long and short **O** picture cards, Velcro, hole punch, picture board, sound muncher

Punch a hole at the top of each long and short **O** picture card and hot glue a piece of Velcro to the back. Hot glue the matching piece of Velcro on the overalls or the on-off switch.

Hang the overalls and the on-off switch on the wall where the children can see and touch them. Place the opossum by the overalls and the octopus by the on-off switch.

Gather the children by the opossum, overalls, octopus, on-off switch, and the picture board.

Short O

Tell the children: "I would like you to meet Officer Octopus. Officer Octopus always turns lights off when no one is in a room to save electricity. He makes a special ŏ–ŏ–ŏ–ŏ sound when he flips the on-off switch to off. (Have the children pretend to turn off switches and make the short sound.) Officer Octopus has brought in his on-off light switch from his home today because he needs out help decorating it with pictures that begin with the short **O** sound. Can you help Officer Octopus decorate his on-off switch with pictures that begin with the same sound as octopus, on, off, and the special sound Officer makes, ŏ–ŏ–ŏ–ŏ?"

As you point to each picture on the board, the children name the object. Repeat the word, emphasizing the beginning sound of each word. Call the children one at a time to come up to the picture board and pick out a card. If the picture begins with a short **O** sound, he/she sticks it on the on-off switch. Have Officer Octopus and the children make the short sound each time a new short **O** picture is added to the on-off switch.

Introducing the Letter O o *(cont.)*

Sounds and Pictures *(cont.)*

Long O

Tell the children: "I would like you to meet Oakie Opossum. Oakie Opossum loves to climb and hang by his tail from oak trees. That is why his friends call him Oakie. Oakie always wears overalls every day. When he puts on his overalls in the morning he makes a special ō–ō–ō–ō sound. (Have the children pretend to put on a pair of overalls while making the long sound.) Oakie has brought his overalls with him today because he needs our help. He thinks his overalls are looking too old. He wants us to make his overalls look better by decorating them with pictures that begin with the long O sound. Can you help Oakie Opossum decorate his overalls with pictures that begin with the same sound as opossum, overalls, and the special sound Oakie makes whenever he puts on his overalls, ō–ō–ō–ō?"

As you point to each picture on the board, the children name the object. Repeat the word, emphasizing the beginning sound of each word. Call the children one at a time to come up to the picture board and pick out a card. If it begins with a long O, the child sticks it on the overalls while Oakie and the children make the long sound.

Leave the overalls, opossum, the on-off switch, and octopus out in the classroom.

After you have done this activity a few times, mix up the pictures on the overalls and the on-off switch.

Tell the children: "All of the pictures fell off of the overalls and the on-off switch, and Oakie and Officer Octopus tried to put them back in the proper places, but they are not sure if they did it correctly. Ask the children to look at the overalls and the on-off switch to see if any pictures need to be changed from the long O overalls to the short O on-off switch and vice versa.

If you want to challenge your class even more, stick some non–O cards on both the overalls and the on-off switch. Tell the children that the U pictures were mixed up with other picture cards. When the children find a non–O picture card on the oar or on-off switch, have them feed it to the sound muncher. The children make the beginning sound of the non–O picture as the sound muncher eats it.

Introducing the Letter O o *(cont.)*

Sounds and Objects

Long O

Materials: a piece of blue poster board cut to resemble the ocean, objects that begin with the long O sound (oatmeal, over coat, over shoes, can opener, oak leaves, ovals, "open" sign)

Short O

Materials: large, laminated desk top paper calendar of the month of October, objects that begin with the short O sound (olives, picture of ostrich, picture of ox, toy octopus, opera glasses, odd numbers)

Place the ocean and calendar page on the floor. Mix up the short and long O objects and place them on the ocean and calendar. Have the children name each object as you show it to the class. Repeat the word, emphasizing the beginning sound. As the objects are introduced to the class, place them on a table.

Each child comes up to the table and selects an object. If it begins like October, the child places it on the calendar of October. If it begins like ocean, he/she places it on the ocean.

When you feel that the children can distinguish between the long and short O sounds, you may decide to challenge them by adding into the group objects that begin with other sounds. If a child picks up one of these objects, he/she can feed it to the sound muncher. The child or the class makes the beginning sound of the non-O object that is being eaten.

Letter Centers

Office

Materials: office supplies and equipment: papers, paperclips, staplers, typewriters, telephone, etc.

Children pretend to work in an office.

O o Play Dough

Materials: play dough, cookie cutters in shapes that begin with the long and short letter O (oak leaf, octopus, etc.)

Children press cookie cutter numbers and pictures into the play dough to make pictures and patterns. They can also roll out the dough to form the capital and lowercase letter O o.

Ocean

Materials: paper, crayons or paints, pictures of ocean life

Children draw or paint an ocean and fill it with various kinds of ocean life.

Introducing the Letter O o *(cont.)*

Let's Learn

Have the children tell you which word or words begins with a long or short **O** sound in each question or command that you read to them. Write the long and short **O** words on a wall chart or on the chalkboard.

Let's Talk

- Name something that you might see in the month of October. (trick or treaters, falling leaves, pumpkins)
- Name an odd number. (one, three, five, seven, etc.)
- Name something that you have to turn on before you can use it. (oven, television, iron)
- Give an example of an opposite. (hot-cold, white-black, up-down)
- Name something that lives in the ocean. (whale, shark, octopus, shrimp)
- Name something that you can open. (door, can, gift, mail)

Let's Move

- Move around the room like an octopus, ostrich, otter, and opossum.
- Climb an oak tree.

Let's Pretend

Pretend to:
- put on a pair of overalls
- eat a bowl of oatmeal
- play the oboe

Let's Do

- Count any **O**-shaped cereal out to correspond with oral or written numbers.
- Record how old the children are on a bar graph.
- Make up a class tongue twister using long **O** words: *Opal ate oatmeal while oaring over the ocean.*
- Make up a class tongue twister using short **O** words: *The octopus' old office smelled like oily olives.*

Introducing the Letter O o *(cont.)*

Short O Picture Cards   **Long O Picture Cards**

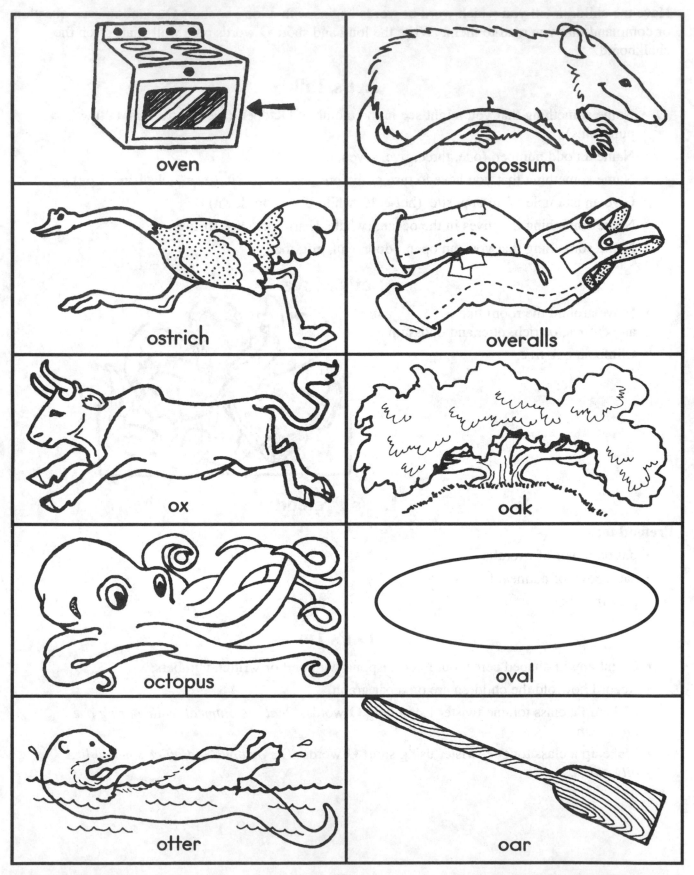

oven

opossum

ostrich

overalls

ox

oak

octopus

oval

otter

oar

Introducing the Letter O o *(cont.)*

Patterns

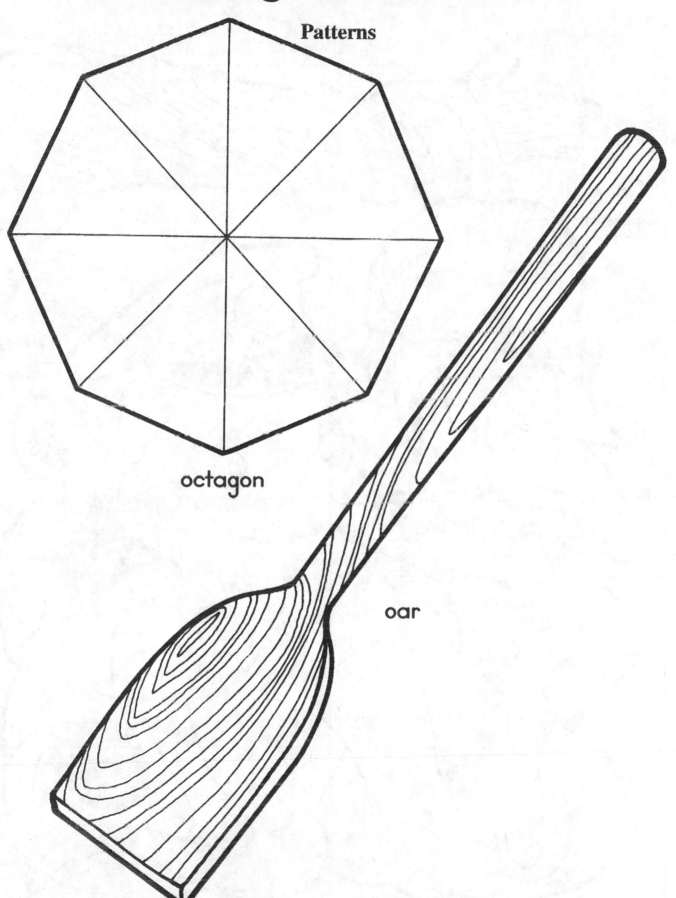

octagon

oar

Introducing the Letter O o (cont.)

Patterns

Oakie
Opossum

Officer
Octopus

Introducing the Letter P p

Letter P Literature: *The Rain Puddle* by Adelaide Holl

After reading *The Rain Puddle*, name all of the animals in
the story. Ask the children to explain why the animals were
mistaken about what was actually in the puddle. Talk about
reflections, and compare the puddle to a mirror. Ask what
happened to the puddle when the sun came out (it
evaporated). Cut a big piece of construction paper into a
circle that resembles a puddle. Gather the children around the "puddle" and let them draw a picture of
what they would see if they looked in a real puddle.

What Do You Hear?

Materials: letter **P** picture cards (reproduce, color and laminate)

Talk about the sound that the letter **P** makes. Show the children each picture card and ask them to
name each object. Repeat the word, emphasizing the **P** sound.

Give each card to a child. Pick one child to come up in front of the class. That child shows the rest of
the class the picture card he/she is holding. The class responds with the chant

Class: "Panda, panda, what do you hear?" (The student in the front of the class looks at the remaining
pictures and calls on one.)

Child: "I hear pancake beginning like me."

Class: "Pancake, pancake, what do you hear?"

Child: "I hear pencil beginning like me."

Continue until all of the picture cards have been called. The last child responds: "I hear the letter **P**
beginning with me."

The class adds: "We all hear the **P** sound going p–p–p–p!"

P Is a Perfect Letter!

Materials: several large pieces of construction paper or poster board, with a large capital and lowercase
P printed on each, glue, **P** items (pretzels, popcorn, pamphlets, pink and purple paper, postcards,
pennies, price tags, peanuts, pebbles, pipe cleaners, small packets of pepper, paper clips)

Divide the class into groups of four or five. The children work together to glue the **P** items over the
P p. When the glue dries, display the pictures on a bulletin board or wall.

Introducing the Letter P p *(cont.)*

Bulletin Board

Materials: crayons or markers, paper, scissors, magazines, copies of picture cards or other **P** worksheets, glue, blank index cards

Make a large postcard from construction paper or poster board. Write the following directions on it: *Please decorate a paper postcard with pretty pictures that begin with the letter P.*

Staple the postcard to the center of the bulletin board. Show the bulletin board to the children and explain the directions to them.

Give each child an index card as a postcard. Ask the children to decorate their postcards with pictures that begin with the letter **P**, using pictures that they have drawn, pictures cut from magazines, or worksheets that they have colored. Staple their finished postcards to the bulletin board.

The children can search at home for additional pictures that begin with the letter **P** to be added to the bulletin board.

Sounds and Pictures

Materials: panda (stuffed one or reproduced, colored, and laminated panda pattern) pajamas, **P** picture cards, some non–**P** picture cards, Velcro, hole punch, picture board, sound muncher

Punch a hole at the top of each picture card and hot glue a piece of Velcro to the back of each picture card. Hot glue the matching Velcro pieces to the pajamas.

Place most of the **P** picture cards and some non–**P** picture cards on the picture board. Save a few **P** picture cards and several non–**P** picture cards to be added later.

Hang the pajamas on the wall where the children can see and touch them. Place the panda by the pajamas.

Gather the children by the panda, pajamas, picture board, and sound muncher.

Introducing the Letter P p *(cont.)*

Sounds and Pictures *(cont.)*

Tell the children: "I would like you to meet Perfect Panda. Perfect Panda is quite a picky panda. Perfect has to have everything just perfect! She is especially picky about her pajamas. Whenever she puts on or takes off her pajamas she makes a proud p–p–p–p sound. (Have the children pretend to put on a pair of pajamas and make the sound p–p–p–p sound like Perfect Panda.) She has brought a pair of her pajamas with her today because she needs our help. She wants us to help her decorate her pajamas with pretty pictures that begin with the letter **P** so her pajamas with look positively perfect. Can you help her decorate her pajamas with pictures that start with the same sound as panda, pajamas, and the sound that Perfect Panda makes when she puts on her pajamas, p–p–p–p?"

As you point to each picture on the board, the children name the object. Repeat the word, emphasizing the beginning sound of each picture card.

Call the children one at a time to come up to the picture board and pick out a card. If it begins with a **P**, have them stick it on the pajamas while Perfect Panda and the children make the special p–p–p–p sound. If it does not begin with a **P**, have them stick it in the sound muncher. The child or the class makes the appropriate beginning sound while the picture is being eaten.

Leave Perfect Panda and her pajamas out in the classroom. After you have done this activity several times, mix up the pictures on the pajamas and add some more **P** pictures and several non–**P** pictures to the pajamas.

Tell the children: "Perfect Panda added some more pictures to her pajamas, but she is not sure if they all begin with the letter **P**."

Point to each picture on the pajamas and have the class say the word with you. Ask the children to identify which pictures need to be removed from the pajamas and fed to the sound muncher. The sound muncher and the children make the beginning sound of the non–**P** picture as it is being eaten.

Sounds and Objects

Materials: piece of paneling, objects that begin with the letter **P** (puzzles pieces, pepper, peanuts, package, pickles, pebbles, paper clips, paddle, pail, peas, pennies, pencils, pens, pins, paint, pear, pedal, purse, prunes, potato chips, powder, plums, putty, piggybank), several non–**P** objects, sound muncher

Place the paneling on the floor. Place all of the **P** and non–**P** objects on the paneling.

Introducing the Letter P p *(cont.)*

Sounds and Objects *(cont.)*

Have the children name each object as you show it to the class. Repeat the word, emphasizing the beginning sound. As objects are named, place them on a table.

Each child comes up to the table, selects an object, and says its name. If it begins like paneling, the child places it on the paneling. If it does not begin like paneling, he/she feeds it to the sound muncher. The child or the class make the beginning sound of the non–**P** object as it is being eaten.

Leave the paneling and all of the **P** objects out as a display in the classroom.

Letter Centers

Plastic Figures

Materials: assortment of plastic figures

Children play with the figures of people and animals.

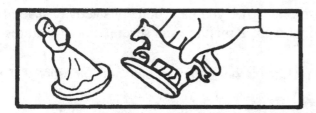

Pink and Purple Pretzel Prints

Materials: pretzels, pink and purple paint, paper

Children dip the pretzels into the paint and press on paper to form a pretty pretzel picture.

Silly Putty

Materials: Silly Putty

Children play, stretch, and mold the Silly Putty.

Puzzles

Materials: various jigsaw puzzles

Children fit together pieces to the puzzles.

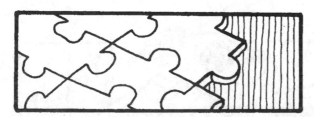

P p Play Dough

Materials: play dough, pencils, pens, paperclips, cookie cutters in shapes that begin with the letter **P** (pumpkin, puppy, pear, etc.)

Children press the **P** objects and cookie cutters into the play dough to make pictures and patterns. They can also roll the dough to form the capital and lowercase letters **P p**.

Let's Learn

Before they respond to each question or direction that you give them, ask the children to identify which word or words begin with a **P**. Write the **P** words on a wall chart or on the chalkboard.

Introducing the Letter P p *(cont.)*

Let's Talk

- Name something that you might find in a purse. (money, mirror, checkbook)
- Name an ingredient that you like to put on pizzas. (cheese, pepperoni, sausage)
- Name a flavor of pudding. (vanilla, chocolate, butterscotch)
- Name something that you can make out of potatoes. (mashed potatoes, French fries, hash browns, etc.)
- Name something that you like to put on pancakes. (butter, syrup, whipped cream)
- Name something that you would find at a birthday party. (cake, presents, balloons)
- Name something that you would see in a parade. (clowns, horses, fire engines)
- Name something that has a pedal on it. (bike, sewing machine, organ, etc.)

Let's Move

- Move around the room like a pony, penguin, pig, panda, and puppy.
- Fly around the room like a parrot, pigeon, and peacock.

Let's Pretend

Pretend to:

- pack your suitcase
- paddle down a stream
- paint a wall
- eat pastry, popcorn
- make a peanut butter and jelly sandwich
- play the piano
- pick pansies

Let's Do

- Count pretzel sticks to correspond with oral or written numbers.
- Children pick their favorite flavor of pudding: vanilla, chocolate, or butterscotch. Record their responses on a "Pudding Graph."
- Make up a tongue twister using **P** words: *Pretty Panda put postcards, pickles, and pudding in her purse.*

	KIM	JACK	LINDA	SIMON	DENISE	TONY	BEV
VANILLA PUDDING	☺			☺			
CHOCOLATE PUDDING		☺	☺			☺	
BUTTERSCOTCH PUDDING					☺		☺

Introducing the Letter P p (cont.)

Letter P Picture Cards

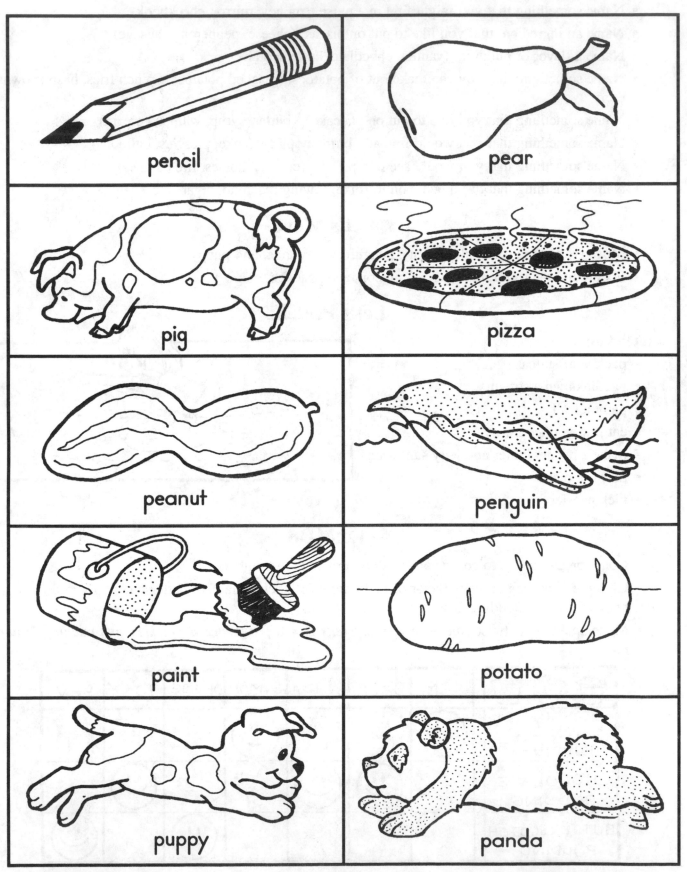

pencil

pear

pig

pizza

peanut

penguin

paint

potato

puppy

panda

Introducing the Letter P p *(cont.)*

Patterns

Perfect Panda

Introducing the Letter Q q

Letter Q Literature: *The Quilt Story* by Tony Johnston and Tomie de Paola

Show the children the cover of *The Quilt Story*. Have a child locate the letter **Q** in the title. Point to the quilt on the bed ans ask the children if they have a favorite quilt or blanket at home. After reading the story ask the following questions:

- Who made the quilt for Abigail? (her mother)
- What are some of the things Abigail did with her quilt? (wrapped it around her, had a tea party, pretended it was a gown, hid under it, and slept under it)
- What types of animals made the quilt their home after it was put in the attic? (mice, a raccoon, and a cat)
- What did Abigail's mother do to make the quilt like new again? (patched the holes, pushed fresh stuffing in, and stitched across the quilt)

What Do You Hear?

Materials: letter **Q** picture cards: reproduced, colored, and laminated

Talk about the sound that the letter **Q** makes. Show the children each picture card and ask them to name each object. Repeat the word, emphasizing the **Q** sound.

Give each card to a child. Pick one child to come up in front of the class. That child will show the rest of the class the picture card he/she is holding. The class responds with the chant "What Do You Hear?"

Class: "Queen, queen, what do you hear?" (The student in the front of the class looks at the remaining pictures and calls on one.)

Child: "I hear quilt beginning like me."

Class: "Quilt, quilt, what do you hear?"

Child: "I hear quarter beginning like me."

Continue until all of the picture cards have been called. The last child responds: "I hear the letter **Q** beginning with me."

The class adds: "We all hear the **Q** sound going q–q–q–q!"

Q Is a Quaint Letter!

Materials: several large pieces of construction paper or poster board with a large capital and lowercase **Q** printed on each, glue, **Q** items ("quarters" cut from aluminum foil, Q-Tips, "quilts" cut from old material, quills)

Divide the class into groups of four or five. The children work together to glue the **Q** items on the **Q q**. When the glue dries, display the pictures on a bulletin board or a wall.

Introducing the Letter Q q *(cont.)*

Bulletin Board

Materials: crayons or markers, scissors, copies of picture cards or other **Q** worksheets, glue, paper plates, aluminum foil

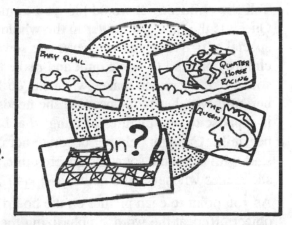

Cut a piece of aluminum foil big enough to cover a paper plate for each child

Cover one paper plate with aluminum foil to resemble a quarter and glue the following directions to it: *Please decorate a quarter with pictures that begin with the letter Q.*

Staple the quarter to the center of the bulletin board. Show the bulletin board to the children and explain the directions to them.

Each child covers a paper plate with a piece of aluminum foil and decorates it with pictures that begin with the letter **Q**, using pictures that they have drawn, pictures cut from magazines, or worksheets that they have colored. Staple their finished quarters to the bulletin board.

The children can search at home for additional pictures that begin with the letter **Q** to be added to the bulletin board.

Sounds and Pictures

Materials: queen (reproduced, colored, and laminated queen all non-**Q** patterns), a quilt (use a baby's quilt), **Q** picture cards, some non-**Q** picture cards, Velcro, hole punch, picture board, sound muncher

Punch a hole at the top of each picture card and hot glue a piece of Velcro to the back. Use hot glue or safety pins to attach the matching Velcro pieces to the quilt.

Place most of the **Q** picture cards and some non-**Q** picture cards on the picture board. Save a few **Q** picture cards and several non-**Q** picture cards to be added later.

Hang the quilt on the wall where the children can see and touch it. Place the queen by the quilt. Gather the children by the quilt, queen, picture board, and sound muncher.

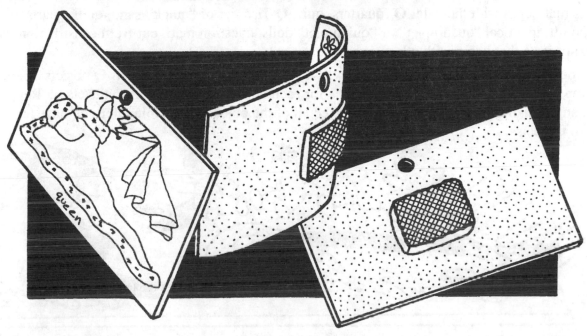

Introducing the Letter Q q *(cont.)*

Sounds and Pictures *(cont.)*

Tell the children: "I would like you to meet Quick Queen. Quick Queen is the quickest quilter in the whole world. She makes a special q–q–q–q sound whenever she sews on her quilts. (Have the children pretend to sew a quilt and make the special q–q–q–q sound like the queen makes when she quilts). "She has brought her quilt with her today because she needs our help. Quick Queen is suppose to sew pictures of things that begin with the letter **Q** on her quilt. Can you help her decorate her quilt with pictures that start with the same sound as queen, quilt, and the special sound she makes whenever she quilts, q–q–q–q?"

As you point to each picture on the board, the children name the object. Repeat the word, emphasizing the beginning sound of each picture card.

Call the children one at a time to come up to the picture board and pick out a card. If it begins with a **Q**, the child sticks the picture on the quilt while Quick Queen and the children make her special sound, q–q–q–q. If it does not begin with a **Q**, he/she feeds it to the sound muncher. The child or the class makes the beginning sound of the non-**Q** picture as it is being eaten.

Leave the quilt and Quick Queen out in the classroom. After you have done this activity several times, mix up the pictures on the quilt and add some more **Q** pictures and several non-**Q** pictures to the quilt.

Tell the children: "Quick Queen added some more pictures to her quilt, but she is not sure if they all begin with the **Q** sound."

Point to each picture on the quilt and have the class say the word with you. Ask the children to look at the quilt and identify any pictures which need to be fed to the sound muncher. The sound muncher and the children make the beginning sound of the non-**Q** picture as it is being eaten.

Sounds and Objects

Materials: large piece of paper or poster board with a question mark written on it (use a wide marker), objects that begin with the letter **Q** (quarters, quiz, Q-Tips, jar of "quick" sand, quill, quarts of milk or juice, quilt, identical "quadruplet" or "quintuplet" dolls, question mark cut from construction paper), several objects that begin with other sounds

Place the paper question mark on the floor. Place all of the **Q** objects and non-**Q** objects on top of the question mark. Have them tell you the name for each object as you show it to the class. Repeat the word, emphasizing the beginning sound. Place all of the objects on a table after you have introduced them to the class.

Introducing the Letter Q q *(cont.)*

Sounds and Objects *(cont.)*

Each child comes up to the table, selects an object, and says its name. If it begins like question mark, the child places it on the question mark. If it does not begin like question mark, he/she feeds it to the sound muncher. The child or the class makes the beginning sound of the non–**Q** object as it is being eaten.

Leave the question mark and all of the **Q** objects out as a display in the classroom.

Letter Centers

Quarters

Materials: quarters (play money), a shallow box of "quick" sand

Children dig for quarters in the sand, count them, and record on a chart how many they found.

Q-Tip Pens

Materials: paint, Q-Tips, paper

Children dip the end of Q-Tips into paint and write the capital and lowercase **Q q** all over their papers.

Quilt

Materials: markers and crayons, paper divided into squares to resemble the patches on a quilt

Children design their own quilts by decorating each section of the paper with markers or crayons.

Q q Play Dough

Materials: play dough, quarters, Q-tips, cookie cutters in shapes that begin with the letter **Q** (queen, quilt, etc.)

Children press quarters, Q-tips, and cookie cutters into the play dough to form pictures and patterns. They can also roll the dough to form the capital and lowercase letters **Q q**.

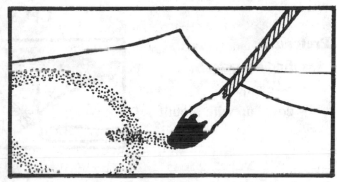

Let's Learn

Before they respond to each question or direction that you give them, ask the children to identify which word or words begin with a **Q**. Write the **Q** words on a wall chart or on the chalkboard.

Introducing the Letter Q q *(cont.)*

Let's Learn *(cont.)*

Let's Talk

- Name something that you can do quickly. (ride bike, run, get dressed)
- Name a place where you should be quiet. (church, library, hospital, theater)
- Name something that you could buy with a quarter. (gum, eraser, pencil)
- What is another name for the word quarrel? (fight, argument, battle, squabble)
- Name a reason why someone should quit smoking. (bad for their health, smells, yellow teeth)
- Name something that makes you quiver. (cold, scary movie, spiders)

Let's Move

- Move around the room like a quail.
- Quickly jump on your right foot, on your left foot, on both feet, then quit.

Let's Pretend

Pretend to:
- find a quarter
- take a quiz
- cover up with a quilt

Let's Do

- Count Q–Tips to correspond with oral or written numbers.
- Cut out five or six different pieces of material into quilt pieces, let the children group the pieces that look alike, and record their findings on a "Quilt Graph."
- Make up a class tongue twister using **Q** words: *Quiet Queen quizzed her quick quail.*

Introducing the Letter Q q *(cont.)*

Picture Cards

question mark

queen

quadruplet

quarter

quart

quill

quail

quilt

quiver

quiz

Introducing the Letter Q q (cont.)

Pattern

Quick Queen

Introducing the Letter R r

Letter R Literature: *Rooster's Off to See the World* by Eric Carle

Materials: rooster pattern, paper feather tail for each child crayons

After reading *Rooster's Off to See the World*, talk about the characters in the story. Who came along with rooster? How many were there of each type of animal? What did they look like? Have each child pick one type of animal from the story (cat, frog, turtle, or fish) and draw that animal on a feather to form the rooster's tail.

What Do You Hear?

Materials: letter **R** picture cards (reproduced, colored, and laminated)

Talk about the sound that the letter **R** makes. Show the children each of the picture cards and ask them to identify each picture. Repeat the word, emphasizing the **R** sound.

Give each card to a child. Pick one child to come up to the front of the class. That child will show the rest of the class the picture card he/she is holding. The class responds with the chant "What Do You Hear?"

Class: "Ring, ring, what do you hear?" (The child in front of the class looks at the remaining pictures and calls on one.)

Child: "I hear rain beginning like me."

Class: "Rain, rain, what do you hear?"

Child: "I hear rabbit beginning like me."

Continue until all of the picture cards have been called. The last child responds: "I hear the letter **R** beginning with me."

The class adds: "We all hear the **R** sound going r–r–r–r!"

R Is a Radiant Letter

Materials: several large pieces of construction paper or poster, board with a large capital and lowercase **R** printed on each, glue, **R** items (rice, ring-shaped cereal, small pieces of rope, receipts, recipes, raisins, red construction paper rectangles)

Divide the class into groups of four or five. The children work together to glue the **R** items on top of the **R r**. When the pictures are dry, display them on a bulletin board or a wall.

Introducing the Letter R r *(cont.)*

Bulletin Board

Materials: crayons, markers, scissors, copies of picture cards or other **R** worksheets, yellow or brown yarn, one copy of the raft pattern on red paper for each child

Make one large copy of the raft and write the following directions on it: *Please help decorate a red raft with pictures that begin with the letter **R**.*

Staple the large raft to the bulletin board. Show the bulletin board to the children and explain the directions to them.

The children cut out their rafts and decorate them with pictures that begin with the letter **R**, using pictures that they have drawn themselves or pictures cut from magazines and from worksheets that they have colored. Cut yarn into pieces to resemble ropes for the rafts. Punch two holes in each raft and have the children string yarn through the holes and knot.

Staple their finished red rafts onto the bulletin board.

The children can search at home for additional **R** pictures to be added to the bulletin board.

Sounds and Pictures

Materials: rabbit (use a stuffed one or reproduced, colored, and laminated rabbit pattern), a long piece of rope, **R** picture cards, some non–**R** picture cards, Velcro, hole punch, picture board, sound muncher

Punch a hole at the top of each picture card and hot glue a piece of Velcro on the back. Hot glue the matching Velcro piece to the rope.

Place most of the **R** picture cards and some non–**R** picture cards on the picture board. Save a few **R** picture cards and several non–**R** picture cards to be added later.

Hang the rope on the wall where the children can see and touch it. Place the rabbit by the rope.

Gather the children by the rope, rabbit, picture board, and the sound muncher.

Introducing the Letter R r *(cont.)*

Sounds and Pictures *(cont.)*

Tell the children: "I would like you to meet Rowdy Rabbit. Rowdy Rabbit is a special rabbit because he does not just hop like other rabbits. Wherever Rowdy Rabbit goes he jumps there with his jump rope while making a rowdy r–r–r–r sound. (Have the children pretend that they are jumping a rope while making the rowdy r–r–r–r sound like Rowdy Rabbit.) He has brought his rope with him today because he needs our help. He wants his rope to be filled with pictures that start with the letter **R**. Can you help him decorate his rope with pictures that start with the same sound as rabbit, rope, and the rowdy sound he makes whenever he jumps rope, r–r–r–r?"

As you point to each picture on the board, the children name the object. Repeat the word, emphasizing the beginning sound. Call the children one at a time to come up to the picture board and pick out a card. If it begins with an **R**, the child sticks it on the rope while Rowdy Rabbit and the children make the special r–r–r–r sound. If it does not begin with an **R**, he/she feeds it to the sound muncher. The child or the class makes the beginning sound of the picture that is being eaten.

Leave the rope and Rowdy Rabbit out in the classroom.

After you have done this activity several times, mix up the pictures of the rope and add some more **R** pictures and several non–**R** pictures to the rope.

Tell the children: "Rowdy Rabbit added some more pictures to his rope, but he is not sure if they all begin with the letter **R**."

Point to each picture on the rope and have the class say the word with you. Ask the children to look at the rope and identify any pictures which need to be fed to the sound muncher. Have the sound muncher and the children make the beginning sound of the non–**R** picture as it is being eaten.

Sounds and Objects

Materials: large rectangular piece of red paper, objects that begin with an **R** (radio, raft, raincoat, rattle, receipt, rose, racket, rake, rack, record, ruffle, recipe, radish, ring, rice, rope, ravioli), several objects that begin with other sounds

Place the rectangle on the floor. Place all of the **R** objects and non-**R** objects on the rectangle. Ask the children to name each object as you show it to the class. Repeat the word, emphasizing the beginning sound. As objects are named, place them on a table.

Introducing the Letter R r (cont.)

Sounds and Objects (cont.)

Each child comes up to the table, selects an object, and says its name. If it begins like rectangle, the child places it on the rectangle. If it does not begin like rectangle, he/she feeds it to the sound muncher. Have the sound muncher make the sound of the non–**R** object as it is being eaten.

Leave the rectangle and all of the **R** objects out as a display in the classroom.

Letter Centers

Rainbow

Materials: crayons, rainbow pictures

Children color a rainbow.

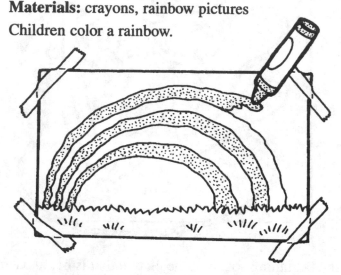

R r Play Dough

Materials: play dough, cookie cutters in shapes that begin with the letter **R** (rainbow, rabbit, reindeer, etc.)

Children press cookie cutters into the play dough to make pictures and patterns. They can also roll out the dough to form the capital and lowercase letters **R r.**

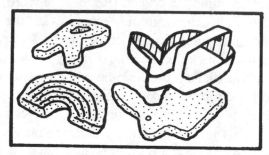

Rubber Band Rubbings

Materials: several different sizes and widths of rubber bands, paper, crayons

Children place paper over rubber bands and rub with a crayon to make patterns.

Pet Rocks

Materials: small rocks, paint or markers

Children paint faces on rocks.

Let's Learn

Have the children tell you which word or words begin with a **R** in each question or command that you read to them. Write the **R** words on a wall chart or on the chalkboard.

Introducing the Letter R r *(cont.)*

Let's Learn *(cont.)*

Let's Talk

- What kind of music do you like to listen to on the radio? (country, jazz, rock)
- Name something that you do when it is raining outside. (color, play a board game, read)
- Name something that you could recycle. (soda cans, milk jugs, newspapers)
- Name something that every person needs to remember. (phone numbers, birth dates, address number, etc.)
- Name your favorite thing to play at recess. (kickball, swing, slide)
- Name something that is in shape of a rectangle. (door, window, shoe box)
- Name something that you might find in a refrigerator. (milk, eggs, cheese)

Let's Move

- Move around the room like a rabbit, rhinoceros, raccoon, and rat.
- Raise your right hand, right foot, right elbow, right shoulder, and right knee.

Let's Pretend

Pretend to:
- rest
- rip a piece of paper, and several pieces of paper
- ride a horse

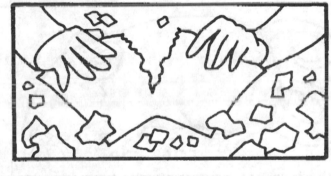

Let's Do

- Count out rubber bands to correspond with oral or written numbers.
- Make up a class tongue twister using **R** words: *Rowdy Rabbit's robe has red roses and ribbons.*

Introducing the Letter R r *(cont.)*

Letter R Picture Cards

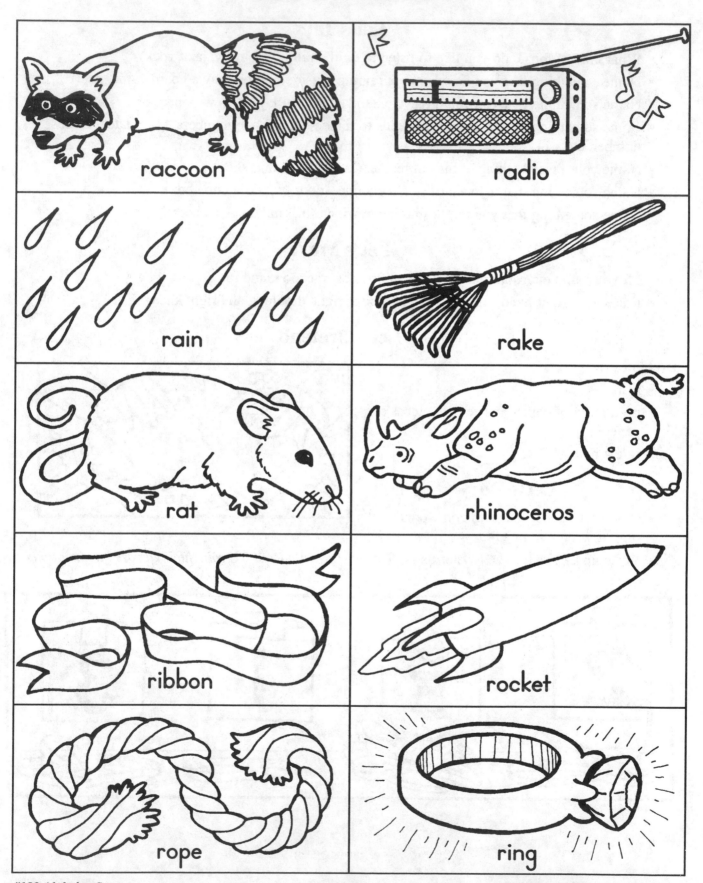

raccoon

radio

rain

rake

rat

rhinoceros

ribbon

rocket

rope

ring

148

Introducing the Letter R r *(cont.)*

Patterns

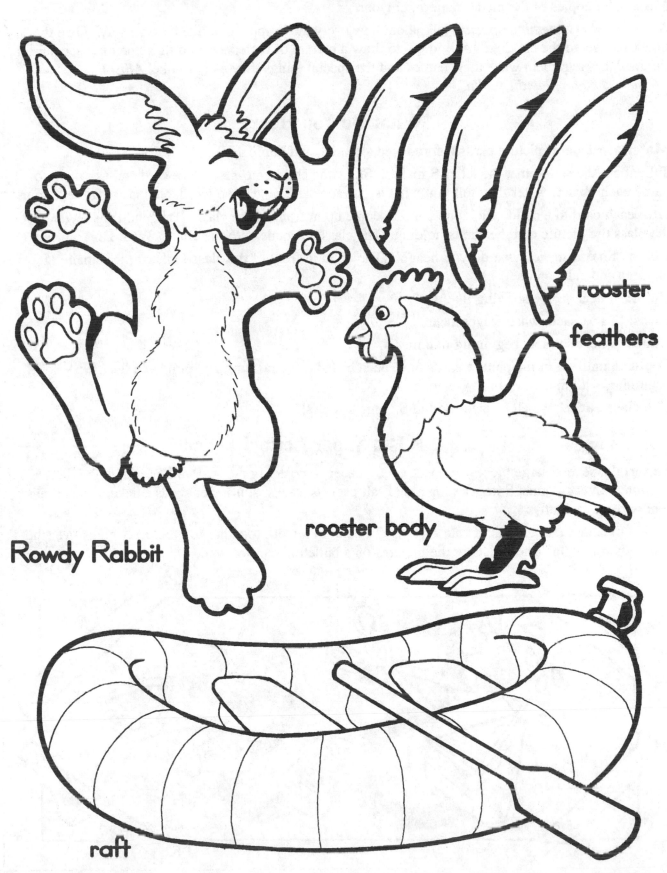

rooster
feathers

Rowdy Rabbit

rooster body

raft

Introducing the Letter S s

Letter S Literature: *Something Special* by David McPhail

Materials: copies of the medal pattern, crayons

After reading *Something Special*, talk about how everyone is special in his/her own way. Give the blank medals to the children. Ask them to draw a picture of themselves doing something special on the medal. Help them write their names and the special things they can do, like: *Allison is special because she can play the violin.*

What Do You Hear?

Materials: letter **S** picture cards (reproduced, colored, and laminated)

Talk about the sound that the letter **S** makes. Show the children each picture card and ask them to name each object. After they tell you what is on each card, repeat the word, emphasizing the **S** sound.

Give each card to a child. Pick one child to come up in front of the class. That child shows the rest of the class the picture card he/she is holding. The class responds with the chant "What Do You Hear?"

Class: "Snake, snake, what do you hear?" (The child in front of the class looks at the remaining pictures and calls on one.)

Child: "I hear sack beginning like me."

Class: "Sack, sack, what do you hear?"

Child: "I hear scissors beginning like me."

Continue until all of the picture cards have been called. The last child responds: "I hear the letter **S** beginning with me."

The class adds: "We all hear the sound **S** going s–s–s–s!"

S Is a Super Letter!

Materials: several large pieces of construction paper or poster board, with a large capital and lowercase **S** printed on each, glue, **S** items (sugar and salt packets, sacks, sunflower seeds, stickers, sugar cubes, sandpaper, spaghetti)

Divide the class into groups of four or five. The children work together to glue the **S** items over the **S s**. When the glue dries, display the pictures on a bulletin board or wall.

Introducing the Letter S s *(cont.)*

Bulletin Board

Materials: crayons or markers, paper, scissors, copies of picture cards or other S worksheets, glue, construction paper, stamp pattern

Make one large copy of the stamp and write the following directions on it: *Please help decorate a sticky stamp with pictures that begin with letter S.*

Staple the stamp in the center of the bulletin board. Show the bulletin board to the children and explain the directions to them.

The children cut out their stamps and decorate them with pictures that begin with the letter S, using pictures they have drawn, pictures cut from magazines, or worksheets they have colored. Staple their finished stamps to the bulletin board.

The children can search at home for additional S pictures to be added to the bulletin board.

Sounds and Pictures

Materials: the skunk and skateboard patterns (reproduced, colored, and laminated), S picture cards, some non–S picture cards, Velcro, hole punch, picture board, sound muncher

Punch a hole at the top of each picture card and hot glue a piece of Velcro to the back. Hot glue the matching Velcro pieces to the skateboard.

Hang the skateboard on the wall where the children can see and touch it. Place the skunk by the skateboard.

Gather the children by the skateboard, skunk, picture board, and sound muncher.

Tell the children: "I would like you to meet Smiling Skunk. Smiling Skunk loves to ride his skateboard wherever he goes. Smiling makes a silly s–s–s–s noise when he rides on his skateboard. (Have the children pretend to ride on a skateboard while they make the s–s–s–s sound like Smiling.) He has brought his skateboard with him today because he needs our help. He thinks that his skateboard would look super if you could help him decorate it with pictures that begin with the letter S. Can you help him decorate his skateboard with pictures that start with the same sound as Skunk, skateboard, and the sound he makes when he is riding on his skateboard, s–s–s–s?"

Introducing the Letter S s *(cont.)*

Sounds and Pictures *(cont.)*

As you point to each picture on the board, the children name the object. Repeat the word, emphasizing the beginning sound. Call the children one at a time to come up to the picture board and pick out a card. If it begins with an **S**, the child sticks it on the skateboard while Smiling Skunk and the children make his silly noise s–s–s–s. If it does not begin with an **S**, the child feeds it to the sound muncher. The child or the class makes the beginning sound of the non–**S** picture as it is being eaten.

Leave the skateboard and Smiling Skunk out in the classroom. After you have done this activity several times, mix up the pictures on the skateboard and add some more **S** pictures and several non–**S** pictures to the skateboard.

Tell the children: "Smiling Skunk added some more pictures to his skateboard, but he is not sure if they all begin with the **S** sound."

Point to each picture on the skatebord and have the class say the word with you. Ask the children to identify which pictures need to be removed from the skateboard and fed to the sound muncher. The sound muncher and the children make the beginning sound of the non–**S** picture as it is being eaten.

Sounds and Objects

Materials: a large square of poster board, objects that begin with the letter **S** (scissors, scarf, scale, sauce, sardines, sandpaper, sandal, sand, salmon, sack, salt, sugar, rubber snake, soap, sponge, stick, screws, stamp, spoon), several non–**S** objects, sound muncher

Place the square on the floor. Place all of the **S** and non–**S** objects on the square. Ask the children to name each object as you show it to the class. Repeat the word, emphasizing the beginning sound. As objects are named, place them on a table.

Each child comes up to the table, selects an object, and says its name. If it begins like square, the child places it on the square. If it has a different beginning sound, the child feeds it to the sound muncher. Have the sound muncher and the children make the sound of the non–**S** object as it is being eaten.

Leave the square and all of the **S** objects out as a display in the classroom.

Introducing the Letter S s *(cont.)*

Letter Centers

Stamps and Stickers

Materials: paper, an assortment of stamps and colored stamp pads, stickers

Children make pictures using stickers and pressing stamps in different colored ink.

Scissors

Materials: scissors, coupons from newspapers and magazines

Children cut out coupons with their scissors.

Seasons

Materials: four boxes labeled winter, spring, summer, fall pictures, and items for each season (winter: snow, mittens, shovel, spring: flowers, rain, umbrella, baby animals, summer: sun, swimming suit, pool, sandals, fall: colored leaves, pumpkins, rake, jacket, football)

Children sort pictures and items according to the four seasons.

S s Play Dough

Materials: play dough, scissors, sandpaper, cookie cutters in shapes that begin with the letter S (sun, seahorse, Santa, etc.)

Children press scissors, sandpaper, and cookie cutters into the play dough to make pictures and patterns. They can also roll out the dough to form the capital and lowercase letters S s.

Will It Sink?

Materials: tub of water, various small items that will sink and some that will float, pencil, paper with all of the items drawn or listed

Children predict whether each item will sink or float. They record their predictions on paper, putting an S by items they think will sink and an F by items they think will float. They put the items in the water and mark how many they correctly predicted.

Let's Learn

Before they respond to each question or direction that you give them, ask the children to identify which word or words begin with an S. Write the S words on a wall chart or on the chalkboard.

Introducing the Letter S s *(cont.)*

Let's Talk

- What is your favorite subject in school? (math, reading, science)
- What is something that makes you sad?
- Describe how sandpaper feels. (rough, bumpy, gritty)
- Name a type of sandwich. (peanut butter and jelly, tuna fish, ham, bologna)
- What is something that you like to do on Saturdays? (watch cartoons, read, play, spend time with family)
- Name something that is salty. (pretzels, potato chips, peanuts, olives)
- Name something that you like to share with a friend. (toys, secret, food, candy)
- Name something that you could find in the sea. (ship, whale, shark, shrimp, seaweed)
- Name a season. (winter, spring, summer, fall)
- Name something that has a seatbelt. (car, grocery cart, airplane seat, baby seat)
- Name a type of soup. (chicken noodle, tomato, clam chowder, vegetable)

Let's Move

- Move around the room like a snake, skunk, shark, seal, sheep.
- Move your right and left shoulders up and down slowly and then fast.
- Skip around the room.

Let's Pretend

Pretend to:

- make a submarine sandwich
- make a sundae
- scoop strawberry sherbet
- catch a salmon
- saddle a horse

- make a sandcastle
- load a grocery sack
- swim
- tie your shoe
- stir sugar into a cup of tea, then take a sip

Let's Do

Count sugar cubes to correspond with oral or written numbers.

Take a survey of the children's favorite sandwich fillings—peanut butter, jelly, tuna, turkey, ham, etc. Record the results on a "Sandwich Graph."

Make up a class tongue twister using **S** words: *Smiling skunk sat on a sticky strawberry sucker.*

Introducing the Letter S s *(cont.)*

Letter S Picture Cards

salt

sandwich

saw

scissors

soap

sponge

squirrel

sun

seahorse

seal

#189 Alphabet Soup

Introducing the Letter S s *(cont.)*

Patterns

stamp

medal

Smiling Skunk

skateboard

156

Introducing the Letter T t

Letter T Literature: *The Giving Tree* by Shel Silverstein

Materials: copies of the tree pattern, crayons, magazines for cutting

Before reading *The Giving Tree* to the children, ask them what a tree could possibly give to someone. After reading the story, list the things that the boy liked to do with the tree at the beginning of the story: climb her, play with her leaves, swing from her branches, eat apples. Talk about the things that the tree gave to the boy as he grew older: apples (money), branches (house), trunk (boat).

Talk about things we use every day that come from trees. Ask the children to draw or cut and glue pictures of furniture, houses, pencils, paper, books, etc., on their trees.

What Do You Hear?

Materials: letter **T** picture cards (reproduced, colored, and laminated)

Talk about the sound that the letter **T** makes. Show the children each picture card and ask them to name each object. Repeat the word, emphasizing the **T** sound.

Give each card to a child. Pick one child to come up in front of the class. That child shows the rest of the class the picture card he/she is holding. The class responds with the chant "What Do You Hear?"

Class: "Towel, towel, what do you hear?" (The child in front of the class looks at the remaining pictures and calls on one.)

Child: "I hear turtle beginning like me."

Class: "Turtle, turtle, what do you hear?"

Child: "I hear taco beginning like me."

Continue until all of the picture cards have been called. The last child responds: "I hear the letter **T** beginning with me. The class adds: "We all hear the **T** sound going t–t–t–t!"

T Is a Terrific Letter!

Materials: several large pieces of construction paper or poster board, with a large capital and lowercase **T** printed on each, glue, **T** items (tape, tags, soda can tabs, tea bags, golf tees, tuna can labels, tic-tac-toe game, tissues)

Divide the class into groups of four or five. The children work together to glue the **T** items over the **T t**. When the glue dries, display the pictures on a bulletin board or wall.

Introducing the Letter T t *(cont.)*

Bulletin Board

Materials: crayons, markers, paper, scissors, copies of picture cards or other **T** worksheets, copies of the T-shirt pattern for each child

Make one large copy of the T-shirt pattern and write the following directions on it: *Please help decorate a T-shirt with terrific pictures that begin with the letter T.*

Staple the T-shirt to the center of the bulletin board. Show the bulletin board to the children and explain the directions to them.

Ask the children to cut out their T-shirts and decorate them with pictures that begin with the letter **T**, using pictures they have drawn, or pictures cut from magazines, or worksheets they have colored. Staple their finished T-shirts on the bulletin board.

The children can search at home for additional pictures that begin with the letter **T** to be added to the bulletin board.

Sounds and Pictures

Materials: the tiger pattern (reproduced, colored, and laminated), large plain tablecloth, **T** picture cards, some non–**T** picture cards, Velcro, hole punch, picture board, sound muncher

Punch a hole at the top of each picture card and hot glue a piece of Velcro to the back of each picture card. Hot glue the matching piece of Velcro to the tablecloth.

Hang the tablecloth on the wall where the children can see and touch it. Place the tiger by the tablecloth.

Gather the children by the tiger, tablecloth, picture board, and sound muncher.

Tell the children: "I would like you to meet Talking Tiger. Talking Tiger loves to talk and sip tea with her friends while sitting by her tablecloth. Talking Tiger does not roar like most tigers, instead she makes a special t–t–t–t sound whenever she talks and sips tea. (Have the children pretend to sip tea while making the t–t–t–t sound like Talking Tiger does.) She has brought her tablecloth with her today because she needs our help. She thinks that her tablecloth would look terrific if it were covered in pictures that start with the letter **T**. Can you help decorate the tablecloth with pictures that start with the same sound as tiger, tablecloth, and the sound she makes when she is talking and sipping her tea, t–t–t–t?"

Introducing the Letter T t *(cont.)*

Sounds and Pictures *(cont.)*

As you point to each picture on the board, the children name the object. Repeat the word, emphasizing the beginning sound. Call the children one at a time to come up to the picture board and pick out a card. If it begins with a T, the child sticks it on the tablecloth while Talking Tiger and the children make the special t–t–t–t sound. If the word does not begin with a T, the child feeds it to the sound muncher. The child or the class makes the beginning sound of the non–T picture as it is being eaten.

Leave the tablecloth and the tiger out in the classroom. After you have done this activity several times, mix up the pictures on the tablecloth and add some more T pictures and several non–T pictures to the children.

Tell the children: "Talking Tiger added some more pictures to her tablecloth, but she is not sure if they all begin with the T sound."

Point to each picture on the tablecloth and have the class say the word with you. Ask the children to look at the tablecloth and identify any pictures which need to be removed and fed to the sound muncher. Have the sound muncher and the children make the beginning sound of the non–T picture as it is being eaten.

Sounds and Objects

Materials: large towel, objects that begin with the letter T (small table, tablespoon, several types of tape, tapioca pudding box, tea bags, tea leaves, teddy bear, golf tee, T-shirt, telephone, telephone book, tambourine, telescope, toothpaste, toothbrush, tools, tomatoes, 1 can of tomato sauce), several non–T objects

Place the towel on the floor and place all of the T and non–T objects on the towel. Have the children name each object as you show it to the class. Repeat the word, emphasizing the beginning sound. As objects are named, place them on a table.

Each child comes up to the table, selects an object, and says its name. If it begins like towel, the child places it on the towel. If it does not begin like towel, he/she feeds it to the sound muncher. The child or the class makes the beginning sound of the non–T object as it is being eaten.

Leave the towel and all of the T objects out as a display in the classroom.

Introducing the Letter T t *(cont.)*

Letter Centers

T t Play Dough

Materials: play dough, cookie cutters in shapes that begin with the letter **T** (turtle, tiger, top, etc.)

Children press cookie cutters into the play dough to make pictures and patterns. They can also roll out the dough to form the capital and lowercase letters **T t**.

Telephone

Materials: dial and push-button telephones; class telephone book with all of the children's names and numbers along with other numbers, such as the school, local restaurants, shops, etc.

Children look up numbers and pretend to talk to friends, place orders, ask questions, etc.

Table

Materials: small table, tablecloth, napkins, play dishes, glasses and silverware, centerpiece

Children set a table, using all of the items included in the center.

Tracing

Materials: tracing paper, pencils, outlines of **T** objects (turtle, tiger, triangle, etc.)

Children lay tracing paper over the **T** outlines and trace.

Toothpick Tents or Teepees

Materials: toothpicks, glue, paper with the outline of a tent or a teepee drawn on it

Children glue toothpicks down on top of the tent or teepee outlines.

Let's Learn

Before they respond to each question or direction that you give them, ask the children to identify which word or words begin with a **T**. Write the **T** words on a wall chart or on the chalkboard.

Let's Talk

- Name your favorite television show.
- Name something that you put in a taco. (meat, cheese, lettuce, sauce)
- Name something that has a tail. (kite, dog, cat, horse, fish, lizard)
- Name a type of toy that you like to play with. (doll, car, board game)
- Name something you do to keep your teeth healthy. (brush; floss; don't eat a lot of candy, soda and sweets; go to the dentist)
- Name something that you like to talk about. (basketball, toys, books, movies)

Introducing the Letter T t *(cont.)*

Let's Move

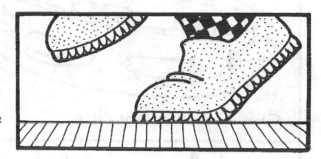

- Tap your feet softly, loudly, slowly, fast.
- Move around the room like a turtle, tiger, tarantula.
- Tiptoe around the room.
- Creat a train. Start by forming a line. Hold the shoulders of the person in front of you. Drive the train around the room.

Let's Pretend

Pretend to:
- put on a T-shirt
- call someone on the telephone
- play a tambourine, and tuba
- set the table (don't forget the tablecloth!)
- make and eat tapioca pudding
- take your temperature
- be a turkey-gobble and strut
- walk on a tight rope

Let's Do

- Count toothpicks out to correspond with oral or written numbers.
- Sort golf tees according to color, record findings on a "Tee Graph."
- Plant a tree, in a pot or in the school yard.
- Make up a class tongue twister using **T** words: *Timmy Turtle travels by taxi, train, and tugboat.*

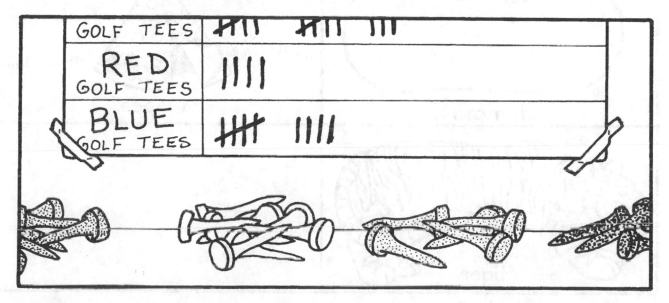

GOLF TEES	卌III 卌II III
RED GOLF TEES	IIII
BLUE GOLF TEES	卌 IIII

Introducing the Letter T t (cont.)

Letter T Picture Cards

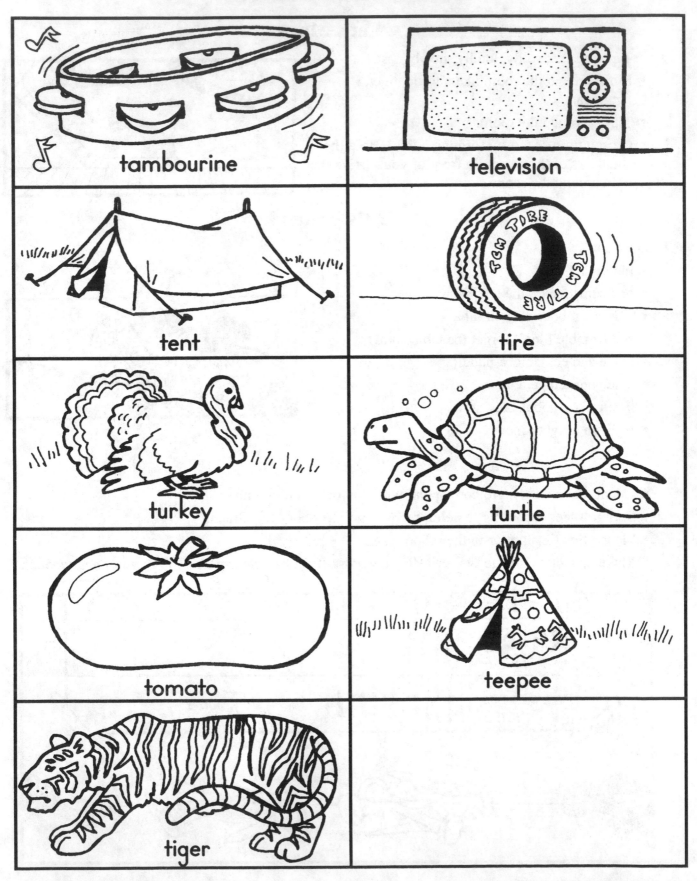

tambourine

television

tent

tire

turkey

turtle

tomato

teepee

tiger

Introducing the Letter T t *(cont.)*

Patterns

T-shirt

tree

Talking Tiger

Introducing the Letter U u

Letter U Literature: *Great Day for Up* by Dr. Seuss

Materials: construction paper, crayons

After reading *Great Day for Up*, talk about some of the things and animals that were up in the story. Re-read the story and count how many times the word "up" is used in the entire story by making tally marks on a wall chart or on the bulletin board (49, including the cover and title page). Have the children draw a picture of things that they would find up in the sky, like kites, stars, birds, clouds, airplanes, etc.

What Do You Hear?

(Long and short sounds may be introduced separately)

Materials: letter long **U** and short **U** pictures cards (reproduced, colored, and laminated)

Working with one set of cards at a time, show the children each picture card and ask them to name the object. Repeat the word, emphasizing the U sound, for example, ŭ–ŭ–ŭ–ŭnder. Talk about the two different sounds that the letter **U** makes. When sounding out the long **U**, tell the children that it says its own name just as it does when they say the alphabet: *T,U,V*. When sounding out the short **U** sound, tell them that is the sound that they make when they can't think of what to say—uh. Have the children practice the long and short **U** sounds.

Give each picture card to a child. Pick one child to come up in front of the class. That child shows the rest of the class the picture card he/she is holding.

The class responds with the chant "What Do You Hear?"

Short U

Class: "Umbrella, umbrella, what do you hear?" (The child in front of the class looks at the remaining pictures and calls on one.)

Class: "Umpire, umpire, what do you hear?"

Child: "I hear umpire beginning like me."

Class: "Undershirt, undershirt, what do you hear?"

Continue until all of the short **U** picture cards have been called. The last child responds: "I hear the letter U beginning with me."

The class adds: "We all hear the short **U** sound going ŭ–ŭ–ŭ–ŭ!"

164

Introducing the Letter U u *(cont.)*

What Do You Hear? *(cont.)*

Long U

Class: "Unicorn, unicorn, what do you hear?

Child: "I hear ukulele beginning like me."

Class: "Ukele, Ukele,, what do you hear?"

Child: "I hear United States beginning like me."

Continue until all of the long **U** picture cards have been called. The last child responds: "I hear the letter **U** beginning with me."

The class adds: "We all hear the long **U** sound going ū–ū–ū–ū!"

U Is a Unique Letter

Materials: several large pieces of construction paper or poster board, with a large capital and lowercase **U** written on each, glue, crayons, **U** items (small paper umbrellas, UPC symbols, plastic utensils, uppercase letters)

Divide the class into groups of four or five. The children work together to glue the **U** items over the **U u**. When the glue dries, display the pictures on a bulletin board or wall.

Bulletin Board

Materials: crayons, markers, paper, scissors, glue, pictures of objects beginning with **U** from the picture card section or other worksheets, construction paper, copies of the United States and umbrella patterns for each child

Make one large copy of the United States pattern and write the following directions on it: *Please decorate the United States with unique pictures that begin with the long U sound.*

Make one large copy of the umbrella pattern and write the following directions on it: *Please decorate an umbrella with unusual pictures that begin with the short U sound.*

Staple the United States and the umbrella to the bulletin board. Show the bulletin board to the children and explain the directions to them.

Have the children cut out the United States and umbrella and decorate the United States with long **U** pictures and the umbrella with short **U** pictures, using pictures that they have drawn themselves, or pictures cut from magazines, or worksheets that they have colored. Staple their finished United States and umbrellas onto the bulletin board.

The children can search at home for additional long and short **U** pictures to be added to the bulletin board.

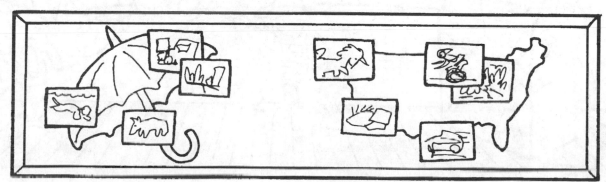

Introducing the Letter U u *(cont.)*

Sounds and Pictures

(For older or more advanced students, short and long sounds may be presented)

Materials: unicorn (use a stuffed one or a reproduced, colored, and laminated unicorn pattern), the unicycle and umpire patterns (reproduced, colored, and laminated), umbrella (use a real one or the reproduced, colored, and laminated pattern), long and short **U** picture cards, Velcro, hole punch, picture board, sound muncher

Punch a hole at the top of each long and short **U** picture card and hot glue a piece of Velcro to the back. Hot glue the matching piece of Velcro to the unicycle or the umbrella.

Mix up the long and short **U** picture cards and hang them on the picture board.

Hang the unicycle and the umbrella on the wall where the children can see and touch them. Place the unicorn by the unicycle and the umpire by the umbrella.

Gather the children by the unicorn, unicycle, umbrella, umpire, and the picture board.

Short U

Tell the children: "I would like you to meet Unhappy Umpire. Unhappy Umpire is unhappy because he thinks his umbrella is ugly. Whenever he puts up his umbrella and looks at it he makes an unusual ŭ–ŭ–ŭ–ŭ sound. (Have the children open up an umbrella and make the short sound like Unhappy Umpire does.) Unhappy Umpire has brought his umbrella with him today because he wants us to change it from an ugly umbrella to a beautifully decorated umbrella filled with pictures that begin with the short U sound. Can you help Unhappy Umpire decorate his umbrella with pictures that start with the same sound as umpire, umbrella, and the unique sound he makes, ŭ–ŭ–ŭ–ŭ?"

As you point to each picture on the board, the children name the object. Repeat the word, emphasizing the beginning sound. Call the children one at a time to come up to the picture board and pick out a card. If the picture begins with a short **U** sound, he/she sticks it on the umbrella. Have Unhappy Umpire and the children make the short **U** sound every time a new short **U** picture is added to the umbrella.

Introducing the Letter U u *(cont.)*

Sounds and Pictures *(cont.)*

Long U

Tell the children: "Unique Unicorn is visiting today. Unique Unicorn is a special unicorn because he can ride a unicycle. Unique makes a unique ū–ū–ū–ū sound whenever he rides his unicycle. (Have the children pretend to ride a unicycle while making the long sound.) Unique Unicorn has brought his unicycle with him today because he needs our help. He wants us to help him decorate his unicycle with pictures that begin with the long **U** sound. Can you help Unique Unicorn decorate his unicycle with pictures that start with the same sound as unicorn, unicycle, and the special sound that he makes, ŭ–ŭ–ŭ–ŭ?"

As you point to each picture on the board, the children name the object. Repeat the word, emphasizing the beginning sound. Call the children one at a time to come up to the picture board and pick out a card. If it begins with a long **U**, the child sticks it on the unicycle while Unique Unicorn and the children make the long **U** sound.

Leave the unicycle, unicorn, umbrella, and umpire out in the classroom.

After you have done this activity a few times, mixup the pictures on the unicycle and the umbrella.

Tell the children: "Unusual Unicorn rode his unicycle by the umbrella and accidentally knocked all of the pictures off his unicycle and the umbrella. He tried to put them back where they belong, but he is not sure if he put them back the right way."

Ask the children to look at the unicycle and the umbrella and identify any pictures that need to be switched from the unicycle to the umbrella or vice versa.

If you want to challenge your class even more, add some non–**U** picture cards to both the unicycle and the umbrella. Tell the children that the **U** pictures were mixed up with other picture cards. When the children find a non–**U** picture card on the umbrella or unicycle, have them feed it to the sound muncher. The children make the beginning sound of the non–**U** picture as the sound muncher eats it.

Introducing the Letter U u *(cont.)*

Sounds and Objects

Long U

Materials: uniform (any type), objects that begin with the long **U** sound (a map or puzzle of the United States, UPC symbols, utensils, utensil tray, toy unicorn)

Short U

Materials: undershirt (large, white man's undershirt), objects that begin with the short **U** sound (umbrella, uppercase letters, umpire's mask)

Place the uniform and the undershirt on the floor. Mix up the long and short **U** objects and place them on the undershirt and uniform. Ask the children to name each object as you show it to the class. Repeat the word, emphasizing the long or short **U** sound at the beginning. As each object is introduced to the class, place it on a table.

Each child comes up to the table, selects an object, and says its name. If it begins like uniform, the child places it on the uniform. If it begins like undershirt, he/she places it on the undershirt.

When you feel that the children can distinguish between the long and short **U** sounds, you may challenge the children by adding into the group objects that begin with other sounds. If a child picks up one of these objects, he/she can feed it to the sound muncher. The child or the class makes the beginning sound of the non–U object that is being eaten.

Letter Centers

Uppercase Letters

Materials: pencils, handwriting papers with uppercase letters written on them

Children trace and write uppercase letters on handwriting paper.

Underground

Materials: paper, crayons

Children draw pictures of things that they could find underground like worms, rocks, ants, groundhog, etc.

United States

Materials: puzzle of the United States

Children work a puzzle of the United States.

U u Play Dough

Materials: play dough, plastic utensils, cookies cutters in shapes that begin with the long and short **U** sounds (umbrella, United States, unicorn, etc.)

Children press utensils and cookie cutters into the play dough to make pictures and patterns. They can also roll out the dough to form the capital and lowercase letters **U u.**

Introducing the Letter U u *(cont.)*

Let's Learn

Before they respond to each question or direction that you give them, ask the children to identify which word or words begin with a U. Write the U words on a wall chart or on the chalkboard.

Let's Talk

- Name someone who wears a uniform to work. (police officer, postman, athlete, nurse)
- Name a type of kitchen utensil. (spatula, strainer, whisk)
- Name a place in the United States that you have been.
- Name something that you might see up in the sky. (sun, birds, clouds)
- Name something that you might find under a rock. (spider, cricket, slug)
- Tell me what makes you unique.

Let's Move

- Walk uphill.
- Usher someone to his/her seat.
- Climb under the table, then get back up.

Let's Pretend

Pretend to:
- ride a unicycle
- play the ukulele
- put up your umbrella because it is starting to rain
- cook using imaginary utensils

Let's Do

- Count out plastic utensils to correspond with oral or written numbers.
- Make up a class tongue twister using long U words: *The unicorn made a U-turn on his unicycle on his way to Utah.*
- Make up a class tongue twister using short U words: *My unhappy uncle the umpire is upstairs unpacking.*

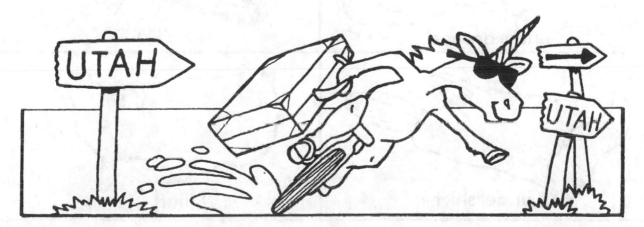

Introducing the Letter U u *(cont.)*

Short U Picture Cards   **Long U Picture Cards**

usher

ukulele

umbrella

uniform

umpire

unicorn

underground

unicycle

undershirt

United States

Introducing the Letter U u *(cont.)*

Patterns

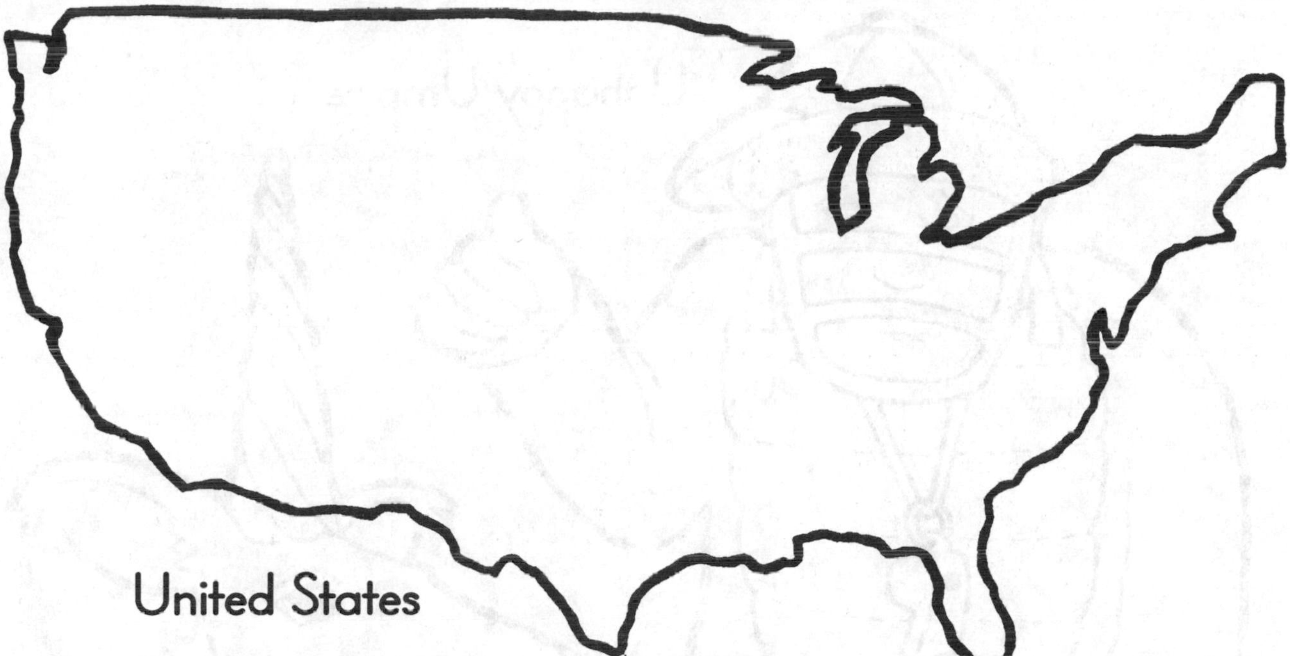

United States

umbrella

Introducing the Letter U u *(cont.)*

Patterns

Unhappy Umpire

Unique Unicorn

unicycle

Introducing the Letter V v

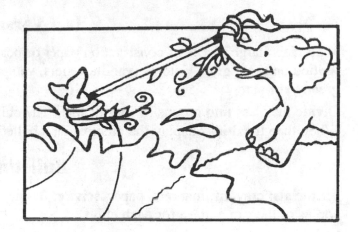

Letter V Literature: *James the Vine Puller* by Martha Bennett Stiles

Materials: construction paper, copies of the elephant and whale patterns for each child, green yarn

After reading *James the Vine Puller,* discuss the story. Ask the following questions:

Where did the story take place?

What things did James like to eat?

What happened to James when he tried to eat coconuts one day?

What happened to James when he tried to eat seaweed?

What was James' plan?

Who won the vine-pulling contest?

The children color and cut out their elephants and whales. Give each child a piece of green yarn as a vine and have him/her tie one end around the elephant's trunk and the other end around the whale's tail. Let the children retell the story in their own words.

What Do You Hear?

Materials: reproduce, color, and laminate the letter **V** picture cards

Talk about the sound that the letter **V** makes. Show the children each picture card and ask them to name the object. Repeat the word, emphasizing the **V** sound.

Give each card to a child. Pick one child to come up in front of the class. That child shows the rest of the class the picture card he/she is holding. The class responds with the chant: "What Do You Hear?"

Class: "Vase, vase, what do you hear?" (The child in front of the class looks at the remaining pictures and calls on one.)

Child: "I hear volleyball beginning like me."

Class: "Volleyball, volleyball, what do you hear?"

Child: "I hear vowel beginning like me."

Continue until all of the picture cards have been called. The last child responds: "I hear the letter **V** beginning with me."

The class adds: "We all hear the **V** sound going v–v–v–v!"

Introducing the Letter V v *(cont.)*

V Is a Versatile Letter!

Materials: large pieces of construction paper or poster board with a large capital and lowercase **V** written on each, glue, **V** items (vanilla wafers, velvet pieces, Valentine candy and cards, brown and green yarn vines)

Divide the class into groups of four or five. The children work together to glue the **V** items on the **V v**. When the glue dries, display the pictures on a bulletin board or a wall.

Bulletin Board

Materials: crayons, markers, paper, scissors, copies of picture cards or other **V** worksheets, glue, copies of the van pattern for each child

Make one large copy of the van and write the following directions on it: *Please decorate a video store's van with a variety of pictures that begin with the letter V.*

Staple the large van to the bulletin board. Show the bulletin board to the children and explain the directions to them.

The children cut out their vans and decorate them with pictures that begin with a **V**, using pictures they have drawn, or cut from magazines, or worksheets they have colored. Staple their finished vans to the bulletin board.

The children can search at home for additional pictures that begin with the letter **V** to be added to the bulletin board.

Sounds and Pictures

Materials: the vulture pattern (reproduced, colored, and laminated), violet vest, **V** picture cards, some non–**V** picture cards, Velcro, hole punch, picture board, sound muncher

Punch a hole at the top of each picture card and hot glue a piece of Velcro to the back. Hot glue the matching piece of Velcro to the vest.

Hang the vest on the wall where the children can see and touch it. Place the vulture by the vest.

Gather the children by the vest, vulture, picture board, and sound muncher.

Introducing the Letter V v *(cont.)*

Sounds and Pictures *(cont.)*

Tell the children: "I would like you to meet Volunteer Vulture. Volunteer Vulture is a very unique vulture because he spends all of his spare time volunteering at a veterinarian's office. Volunteer Vulture always wears his violet vest whenever he volunteers. Volunteer makes a special v–v–v–v sound when he puts on his vest. (Have the children pretend to put on a vest while making the special v–v–v–v sound like Volunteer.) He has brought in his violet vest with him today because he needs our help. He wants us to help him decorate his vest with pictures that start with the letter **V**. Can you help him decorate his vest with the pictures that start with the same sound as vulture, violet vest, and the special sound he makes, v–v–v–v?"

As you point to each picture on the board, the children name the object. Repeat the word, emphasizing the beginning sound of each word. Call the children one at a time to come up to the picture board and pick out a card. If it begins with a **V**, the child sticks it on the vest while Volunteer Vulture and the children make the v–v–v–v sound. If it does not begin with a **V**, have them feed it to the sound muncher. The child or the class makes the beginning sound of the non–V object as it is being eaten.

Leave the vest and Volunteer Vulture out in the classroom.

After you have done this activity several times, mix up the pictures on the vest, and add some more **V** pictures and several non–V pictures to the vest.

Tell the children: "Volunteer Vulture added some more pictures to his vest, but he is not sure they all begin with the **V** sound."

Point to each picture on the vest and have the class say the word with you. Ask the children to identify any pictures which need to be removed and fed to the sound muncher. The sound muncher and the children make the beginning sound of the non–V picture as it is being eaten.

Sounds and Objects

Materials: large piece of velvet, objects that begin with the letter **V**, Valentine card, toy van, vanilla extract bottle, vanilla wafers, vaporizer, Vaseline, vegetable soup, mixed vegetables, veil, vitamins, volleyball, visor, vinegar, video tape, several objects that begin with other letters

Introducing the Letter V v *(cont.)*

Sounds and Objects *(cont.)*

Place the piece of velvet on the floor and place all of the **V** and non–**V** objects on top of it. Have the children name each object as you show it to the class. Repeat the word, emphasizing the beginning sound. As the objects are introduced to the class, place them on a table.

Each child comes up to the table, selects an object, and says its name. If it begins like velvet, the child places it on the velvet. If it does not begin like velvet, he/she feeds it to the muncher. The sound muncher and the children make the beginning sound of the non–**V** object as it is being eaten.

Leave the velvet and all of the **V** objects out as a display in the classroom.

Letter Centers

Velvet and Violet Glitter

Materials: paper, glue, violet glitter, small velvet pieces

Children glue glitter and velvet on paper to make a picture.

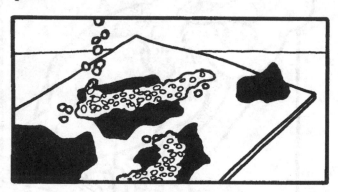

Vegetable Soup

Materials: poster with labeled pictures of vegetables and other ingredients, paper, pencils, crayons

Children create and write their own recipes for vegetable soup and then draw a picture of what it looks like.

V v Play Dough

Materials: play dough, cookie cutters in shapes that begin with the letter **V** (van, Valentines, vase, etc.)

Children press cookie cutters into the dough to form pictures and patterns. They can also roll the dough out to form the capital and lowercase letters **V v.**

Veterinary Center

Materials: stuffed animals, toy doctor kit, bandages

Children examine "sick" animals and treat them with bandages, splints, slings, etc.

Introducing the Letter V v *(cont.)*

Let's Learn

Before they respond to each question or direction that you give them, ask the children to identify which word or words begin with a **V**.   Write the **V** words on a wall chart or on the chalkboard.

Let's Talk

- Name something that has Velcro on it. (shoes, pants, babies' hair bows, coats)
- Name a place where people go on vacation. (to the beach, lake, mountains)
- Name a type of vegetable. (green beans, corn, carrots, squash)
- Name a vowel (a,e,i,o,u)
- Name a person that you like to visit. (neighbor, friend, grandma, aunt)

Let's Move

- Move around the room like a vulture.

Let's Pretend:

Pretend to:
- drive a van
- vacuum the floor
- put on a vest
- climb up and look down a volcano

Let's Do

- Count out Valentine candy to correspond with oral or written numbers.
- Make a list of vegetables.   Have children pick their favorite, and record their answers on a "Vegetable Graph."
- Make up a class tongue twister using **V** words: *The violet van delivered vinegar, vitamins, and vegetables to the vulture.*

Introducing the Letter V v *(cont.)*

Letter V Picture Cards

vacuum cleaner

valentine

van

vulture

vest

vine

violin

volcano

vase

volleyball

Introducing the Letter V v *(cont.)*

Patterns

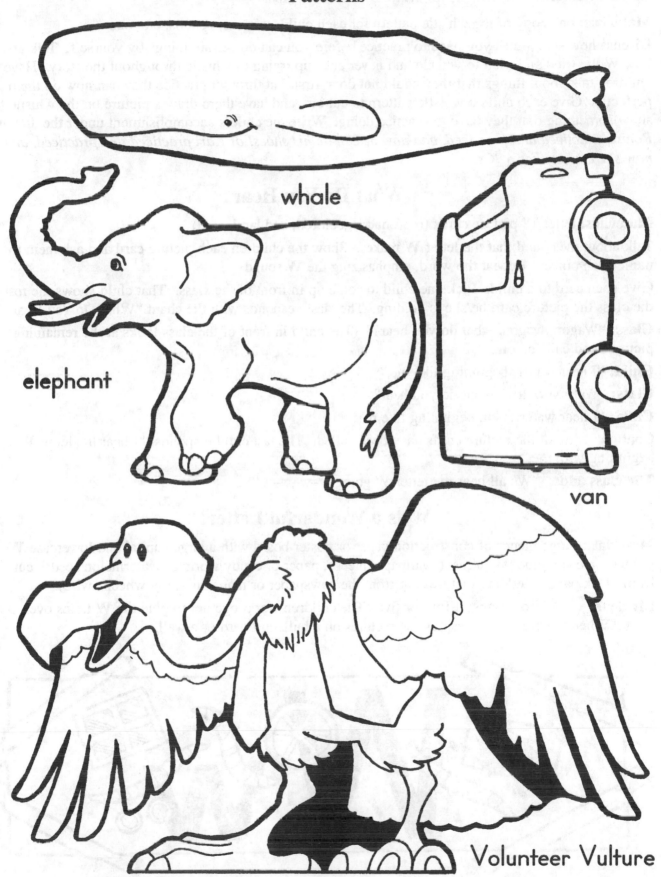

whale

elephant

van

Volunteer Vulture

Introducing the Letter W w

Letter W Literature: *Whistle for Willie* by Ezra Jack Keats

Materials: one copy of the whistle pattern for each child, scissors, pencils, crayons

Discuss how sometimes you have to practice before you can do certain things by yourself. Talk about how Willie tried and tried to whistle and never gave up trying to whistle throughout the story. Have the children talk about things that they could not do at first, but through practice they can now do them perfectly. Give each child a whistle pattern to cut out, and have them draw a picture on the whistle to show something that they have to practice doing. Write the child's accomplishment under the drawing: *Ronnie practiced and practiced, and now he can tie his shoes!* or *Kari practiced and practiced, and now she can say her ABCs!*

What Do You Hear?

Materials: letter **W** picture cards (reproduced, colored, and laminated)

Talk about the sound that the letter **W** makes. Show the children each picture card and ask them to name each object. Repeat the word, emphasizing the **W** sound.

Give each card to a child. Pick one child to come up in front of the class. That child shows the rest of the class the picture card he/she is holding. The class responds with the chant "What Do You Hear?"

Class: "Wagon, wagon, what do you hear?" (The child in front of the class looks at the remaining pictures and calls on one.)

Child: "I hear walrus beginning like me."

Class: "Walrus, walrus, what do you hear?"

Child: "I hear watermelon beginning like me."

Continue until all the picture cards have been called. The last child responds: "I hear the letter **W** beginning with me."

The class adds: "We all hear the letter **W** going w–w–w–w!"

W Is a Wonderful Letter!

Materials: large pieces of construction paper or poster board with a large capital and lowercase **W** printed on each, glue, **W** items (wallpaper pieces, paper or candy worms, "watermelon seeds" cut from black paper, wedding pictures cut from the newspaper or magazines, toy wheels, wire)

Divide the class into groups of four or five. The children work together to glue the **W** items over the **W w**. When the glue dries, display the pictures on a bulletin board or a wall.

Introducing the Letter W w (cont.)

Bulletin Board

Materials: crayons, markers, scissors, copies of picture cards or other **W** worksheets, glue, yarn, hole punch, copies of the wallet pattern for each child

Make one large copy of the wallet and write the following directions on it: *Please help decorate and fill a wallet with wonderful, witty pictures that begin with the letter* **W.**

Staple the large wallet to the center of the bulletin board. Show the bulletin board to the children and explain the directions to them.

The children cut out their wallets, punch holes all around the edges, string yarn through the holes and knot. Using pictures they have drawn, or cut from magazines, or worksheets they have colored, the children glue and draw pictures on the outside, and fill the inside with pictures that begin with the letter **W.** Staple their finished wallets to the bulletin board.

The children can search at home for additional **W** pictures to be added to the bulletin board.

Sounds and Pictures

Materials: witch (use a Halloween decoration or duplicated, colored, and laminated witch pattern), wallpaper, **W** picture cards, several non–**W** picture cards, Velcro, hole punch, picture board, sound muncher

Punch a hole at the top of each picture card and hot glue a piece of Velcro to the back. Hot glue the matching piece of Velcro to the wallpaper.

Place most of the **W** picture cards and some non–**W** picture cards on the picture board. Save a few **W** picture cards and several non–**W** picture cards to be added later.

Hang the wallpaper on the wall where the children can see and touch it. Place the witch beside the wallpaper.

Gather the children by the wallpaper, the witch, the picture board, and the sound muncher.

Tell the children: "I would like you to meet Wacky Witch. Wacky Witch is different from other witches because she does not like to scare people. Wacky Witch spends all of her time hanging wallpaper. When she puts up wallpaper, she is so happy she makes a wonderful w–w–w–w sound. (Have the children make the happy w–w–w–w sound like Wacky while they pretend that they are hanging wallpaper.) She has brought some of her wallpaper with her today because she needs our help. She wants us to decorate her wallpaper with pictures of things that start with the letter **W.** Can you help her decorate her wallpaper with pictures that start with the same sound as witch, wallpaper, and the sound she make when she hangs wallpaper, w–w–w–w?"

Introducing the Letter W w *(cont.)*

Sounds and Pictures *(cont.)*

As you point to each picture on the board, the children name the object. Repeat the word, emphasizing the beginning sound of each word. Call the children one at a time to come up to the picture board and pick out a card. If it begins with a **W**, the child sticks it on the wallpaper while Wacky Witch and the children make the w–w–w–w sound. If the word does not begin with **W**, the child feeds it to the sound muncher. The child or the class makes the beginning sound of the non–**W** picture as it is being eaten.

Leave the wallpaper and the witch out in the classroom. After you have done this activity several times, mix up the pictures on the wallpaper and add some more **W** pictures and several non–**W** pictures to the wallpaper.

Tell the children: "Wacky Witch decided to add some more pictures to her wallpaper, but she is not sure if they all begin with the **W** sound."

Point to each picture on the wallpaper and have the class say the word with you. Ask the children to identify any pictures which need to be removed and fed to the sound muncher. The sound muncher and the children make the beginning sound of the non–**W** picture as it is being eaten.

Sounds and Objects

Materials: wagon, objects that begin with the letter **W** (whale, walrus, watering can, white paper, watch, whistle, watercolors, wheel, watermelon seeds, washcloth, whisk, whipped cream container), several objects that begin with other sounds

Place all **W** objects and non–**W** objects inside the wagon. Have the children name each object as you show it to the class. Repeat the word, emphasizing the beginning sound. As the objects are introduced to the class, place them on a table.

Each child comes up to the table, selects an object, and says its name. If it begins like wagon, the child places it in the wagon. If it does not begin like wagon, he/she feeds it to the muncher. The sound muncher and the children make the beginning sound of the non–**W** object as it is being eaten.

Leave the wagon and all the **W** items out as a display in the classroom.

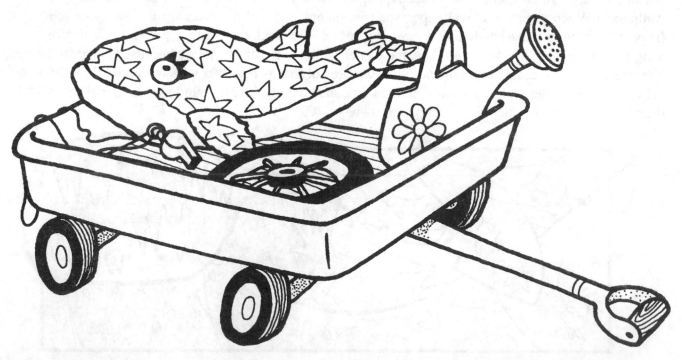

Introducing the Letter W w *(cont.)*

Letter Centers

Wiggle Worms

Materials: paint, paper, paperclips, gummy worms

Children hook gummy worms onto paperclips and wiggle them through paint. They can make different colored worm tracks on their paper.

Window Watching

Materials: crayons, markers, paper

Children draw pictures of what they would see if they looked out windows in their houses, school, or cars.

Wind-up Toys

Materials: an assortment of wind-up toys

Let the children wind up the toys and play!

Weave a Waffle

Materials: glue, light tan paper with precut slits, strips of weaving paper

Children weave paper in and out to make their own waffles. Glue down the ends and let dry. Color glue with brown food coloring for syrup and add a pat of yellow construction paper butter.

W w Play Dough

Materials: play dough, cookie cutters in shapes that begin with the letter **W** (waffles, window, walrus, etc.)

Children press cookie cutters into the dough to make pictures and patterns. They can also roll the dough to form the capital and lowercase letters **W w.**

Let's Learn

Before they respond to each question or direction that you give them, ask the children to identify which word or words begin with a **W.** Write the **W** words on a wall chart or on the chalkboard.

Introducing the Letter W w *(cont.)*

Let's Learn *(cont.)*

Let's Talk

- Can you name something that you often have to add water to before you can eat or drink it? (soup, lemonade, coffee, tea)
- Name something that you wash. (hair, dishes, car, clothes)
- Name things that you like to put on a waffle before you eat it. (butter, syrup, whipped cream, honey)
- Name something that is white. (clouds, sheets, paper, teeth)
- Name something that you wear in the winter. (coat, mittens, boots, scarf)

Let's Move

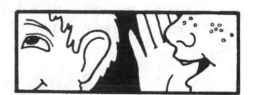

- Waddle around the room.
- Walk over to a friend and whisper something in his/her ear.
- Wiggle like a worm.

Let's Pretend

Pretend to:

- wade in a pond full of water
- weed and water your watermelons in your garden
- whip cream

- wind up a toy, clock, a big robot
- wash your hands, face, hair
- eat a watermelon (spit out the seeds!)
- water a plant

Let's Do

- Count out sugar wafers to correspond with oral or written numbers.
- Place the days of the week in order.
- Make up a tongue twister using **W** words: *Wacky Walrus was washing watermelons on Wednesday.*

Introducing the Letter W w *(cont.)*

Letter W Picture Cards

waffle

wagon

walrus

watch

wing

web

whale

wheel

whistle

windmill

Introducing the Letter W w (cont.)

Patterns

whistle

Wacky Witch

Introducing the Letter X x

Letter X Literature: *The Fox with Cold Feet* by Bill Singer

After reading *The Fox with Cold Feet*, ask the following questions:

What does the fox say throughout the story? ("I'm quick and spry, clever and sly.")

Who does the fox have to help, what does he have to do, and what is his first boot? (sparrow, dig snow to uncover seeds, nest)

Repeat the question for the remaining boots. (second boot—beaver, carries branches, pail; third and forth boot—raccoon, open a garbage can lid, ear muffs and a scarf)

What happens to the fox when he tries to move in all of his boots?

What Do You Hear?

Materials: letter **X** picture cards (reproduced, colored, and laminated)

Talk about the sound that the letter **X** makes. Show the children all of the picture cards. After they tell you what is on each card, repeat the word, emphasizing the *ending* **X** sound.

Give each card to a child. Pick one child to come up in front of the class. That child will show the rest of the class the picture card he/she is holding. The class responds with the chant: "What Do You Hear?"

Class: "Fox, fox, what do you hear?" (The child in from of the class looks at the remaining pictures and calls on one.)

Child: "I hear box ending like me."

Class: "Box, box, what do you hear?"

Child: "I hear ax ending like me."

Continue until all of the picture cards have been called. The last child responds with: "I hear the letter **X** ending with me." The class adds at the end: "We all hear the **X** sound going x–x–x–x!"

X Is an EXcellent Letter!

Materials: several large pieces of construction paper or poster board with a capital and lowercase **X** printed on them, glue, **X** items (small gift boxes, items counted into groups of six, x–rays made of black paper with white chalk bones)

Divide the class into groups of four or five. The children work together to glue the **X** items on the **X x**. When the glue dries, display the pictures on a bulletin board or a wall.

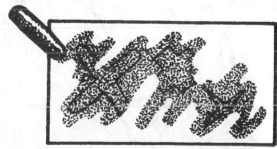

Introducing the Letter X x *(cont.)*

Bulletin Board

Materials: crayons, markers, paper, scissors, glue, magazines, copies of picture cards or other **X** worksheets, copies of the fox pattern for each child

Make one large copy of the fox pattern and write the following directions on it: *Please help decorate a fox with pictures that end with the letter X.*

Staple it in the center of the bulletin board. Show the bulletin board to the children and explain the directions to them.

The children cut out their foxes and decorate them with pictures that end with the letter **X**, using pictures they have drawn themselves, or pictures cut from magazines, or worksheets they have colored. Staple their finished foxes onto the bulletin board.

Sounds and Pictures

Materials: the ox and ax patterns (reproduced, colored, and laminated), **X** picture cards, some non–**X** picture cards, Velcro, hole punch, picture board, sound muncher

Punch a hole at the top of each picture card and hot glue a piece of Velcro to the back. Hot glue the matching Velcro pieces to the ax.

Hang the ax on the wall where the children can see and touch it. Hang the ox by the ax.

Gather the children by the ox, ax, picture board, and sound muncher.

Tell the children: "I would like you to meet Oxie Ox. Oxie Ox loves to chop things down with his ax. Whenever his friends need something chopped down, they have Oxie Ox chop it down with his ax. Oxie makes a special x–x–x–x sound whenever he chops with his ax. (Have the children pretend to chop with an ax while making the x–x–x–x sound like Oxie the Ox does.) He has brought his ax with him today because he needs our help. He thinks his ax will chop faster if it were filled with pictures that end with the letter **X**. Can you help him decorate his ax with pictures that end with the same sound as ox, ax, and the special sound Oxie makes when he is chopping things, x–x–x–x?"

As you point to each picture on the board, the children name the object. Repeat the word, emphasizing the ending sound of each word. Call the children one at a time to come up to the picture board and pick a card that has a picture of something that ends with the letter **X**. If it ends with an **X**, the child sticks it on the ax while Oxie Ox and the children make the x–x–x–x sound. If it does not end with an **X**, he/she feeds it to the sound muncher. The child or the class makes the ending sound of the non–**X** picture as it is being eaten.

Leave the ax and the ox out in the classroom.

Introducing the Letter X x *(cont.)*

Sounds and Pictures *(cont.)*

After you have done this activity several times, add some non–X pictures to the ax.

Tell the children: "Oxie Ox added some more pictures to his ax, but he is not sure if they all end with the letter **X** sound."

Point to each picture on the ax and have the class say the word with you. Ask the children to look at the ax and identify any pictures which need to be removed and fed to the sound muncher. Have the sound muncher and the children make the ending sound of the non–X picture as it is being eaten.

Sounds and Objects

Materials: box, objects that end with the letter **X** (jewelry box, gift box, shoe box, number six cut out of paper, toy ax, toy fox, candle wax, cake mix), several objects that end with other sounds

Place all of the **X** objects and non–X objects inside the box. Have the children name each object as you show it to the class. Repeat the word, emphasizing the ending sound. As objects are named, place them on a table.

Each child comes up to the table, selects an object, and says its name. If it ends like box, the child places it on or in the box. If it does not end like box, he/she feeds it to the sound muncher. The sound muncher and the children make the ending sound of the non–X object as it eats it.

Leave the box and all of the **X** objects out as a display in the classroom.

Letter Centers

X-Rays

Materials: black construction paper, white chalk

Children draw bones with white chalk on the black construction paper.

X Rubbings

Materials: paper, crayons, toothpicks, craft sticks, pipe cleaners

Children make **X** pictures by placing paper over objects that are in the shape of an **X** and rubbing crayons over them.

X's and O's

Materials: tic-tac-toe papers, pencils

Children practice writing the letters **X** and O while playing tic-tac-toe.

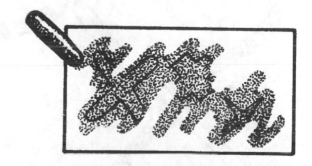

Introducing the Letter X x *(cont.)*

Let's Learn

Before they respond to each question or direction that you give them, ask the children to identify which word or words begin or end with an **X**.   Write the **X** words on a wall chart or on the chalkboard.

Let's Talk

- When would you need to have an x-ray? (dentist exam, broken arm, chest x-ray for pneumonia)
- Name something that you keep in a box. (clothes, toys, a gift, jewelry, shoes)
- Describe a fox (furry, red, sharp teeth)
- Have you ever had chicken pox? Describe what happened to you. (fever, small bumps all over, itchy, take medicine)

Let's Move

- Move around the room like a fox and an ox.
- Make a stack of various-sized boxes. Try to jump over it.

Let's Pretend

Pretend to:
- chop wood, using an ax
- wrap a box and then open it
- be a jack-in-the-box
- mix a cake
- play a xylophone
- to wax the floor, a car

Let's Do

- Shape pipe cleaners in a variety of colors into **X** shapes.
- Children count out the pipe cleaner **X**'s to correspond with oral or written numbers.
- Children sort the pipe cleaners **X**'s according to color and record their findings on an "X Graph."
- Make a tongue twister using words that begin and end in **X**: *Oxie Ox made a box for his fox that has the chicken pox.*

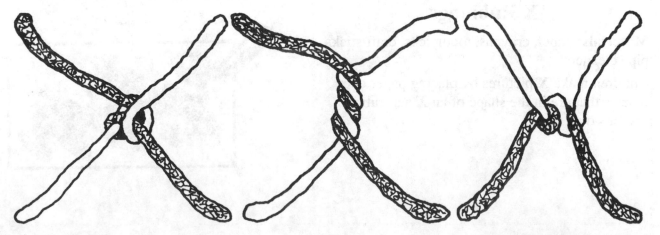

Introducing the Letter X x *(cont.)*

Letter X Picture Cards

fox

box

ax

six

chicken pox

ox

fix

mix

wax

Introducing the Letter X x *(cont.)*

Patterns

fox

ox

ax

Introducing the Letter Y y

Letter Y Literature: *Yertle the Turtle* by Dr. Seuss

Materials: copies of the turtle pattern, crayons, scissors

After reading *Yertle The Turtle,* talk about Yertle's wish to have everything that he could see. List all of the things that he wanted to rule in his land. Discuss what happened to Yertle in the end because of his greed. Have the children talk about things that they have been greedy about: candy, toys, money, food, clothes, etc.

Give each child a turtle to color and cut out. Ask the children to draw or glue pictures on their turtles of things they would like to possess. Staple or tape the turtles on top of each other on a wall. Count how many turtles you have.

What Do You Hear?

Materials: letter Y picture cards (reproduced, colored, and laminated)

Talk about the sound that the letter **Y** makes. Show the children each of the picture cards and ask them to name each object. Repeat the word, emphasizing the **Y** sound.

Give each card to a child. Pick one child to come up in front of the class. That child shows the rest of the class the picture card he/she is holding. The class responds with the chant "What Do You Hear?"

Class: "Yo-yo, yo-yo, what do you hear?" (The child in the front of the class looks at the remaining pictures and calls on one.)

Student: "I hear yak beginning like me."

Class: "Yak, yak, what do you hear?"

Student: "I hear yacht beginning like me."

Continue until all of the picture cards have been called. The last child responds: "I hear the letter **Y** beginning with me."

The class adds: "We all hear the **Y** sound going y–y–y–y!"

Y Is a Yummy Letter!

Materials: large pieces of construction paper or poster board with a large capital and lowercase **Y** printed on each, glue, **Y** items (yellow yarn, yeast, yogurt lids, pocket-sized one-year calendar, label from canned yams)

Divide the class into groups of four or five. The children work together to glue the **Y** items over the **Y y.** When the glue dries, display the pictures on a bulletin board or a wall.

Introducing the Letter Y y *(cont.)*

Bulletin Board

Materials: crayons, markers, paper, scissors, magazines, copies of picture cards or other worksheets, glue, yellow yarn, copies of the yo-yo pattern for each child.

Make one large copy of the yo-yo and write following directions on it: *Please help decorate a yellow yo-yo with pictures that begin with the letter Y.*

Staple it in the center of the bulletin board. Show the bulletin board to the children and explain the directions to them.

Give each child a yo-yo and a piece of yellow yarn long enough to resemble the string on a yo-yo. The children cut out their yo-yos, glue the yellow yarn to the backs, and decorate them with pictures that begin with the letter **Y**. They can use pictures that they have drawn themselves, or pictures cut from magazines or worksheets they have colored. Staple their finished yo-yos on the bulletin board.

The children can search at home for additional **Y** pictures to be added to the bulletin board.

Sounds and Pictures

Materials: (reproduce, color, and laminate the yak pattern), three yardsticks, **Y** picture cards, some non–**Y** picture cards, Velcro, hole punch, picture board, sound muncher

Punch a hole at the top of each picture card and hot glue a piece of Velcro to the back. Hot glue the matching Velcro piece to a yardstick.

Hang the yardsticks on the wall in the shape of a **Y** where the children can see and touch them. Place the yak by the yardsticks.

Gather the children by the yardsticks, yak, picture board, and sound muncher.

Tell the children: "I would like you to meet Yawning Yak. Yawning Yak is different from other yaks because he is always measuring things with his yardstick. Whenever he goes anywhere, he measures everything with his yardstick. Measuring things all the time keeps him very busy and makes him very tired. He makes the most unusual yawny sound while he is measuring: y–y–y–y. (Have the children pretend to measure an object while they make the y–y–y–y sound like Yawning.) He has brought his yardsticks with him today because he needs our help. He wants his yardsticks to be filled with pictures that begin with the letter **Y**. Can you help him decorate his yardsticks with pictures that start with the same sound as yak, yardsticks, and the y–y–y–y sound that Yawning makes when he is measuring things?"

194

Introducing the Letter Y y *(cont.)*

Sounds and Pictures *(cont.)*

As you point to each picture on the board, the children name the object. Repeat the word, emphasizing the beginning sound of each word. Call the children one at a time to come up to the picture board and pick out a card. If it begins with a **Y**, the child sticks it on a yardstick while Yawning Yak and the children make his special sound, y–y–y–y. If it does not begin with a **Y**, he/she feeds it to the sound muncher. The child or the class makes the beginning sound of the non–**Y** picture as it is being eaten.

Leave the yardsticks and Yawning Yak out in the classroom. After you have done this activity several times, mix up the pictures on the yardsticks and add some more **Y** pictures and some non–**Y** pictures to the yardsticks.

Tell the children: "Yawny Yak added some more pictures to his yardsticks, but he is not sure if they all begin with the **Y** sound."

Point to each picture on the yardsticks and have the class say the word with you. Ask the children to look at the yardsticks and identify any pictures which need to be removed and fed to the sound muncher. Have the sound muncher and the children make the beginning sound of the non–**Y** picture as it is being eaten.

Sounds and Objects

Materials: yellow yarn, objects that begin with the letter **Y** (yo-yo, yolk, year, yearbook, yeast, yellow construction paper, yellow pages phone book, yield sign, yogurt, yams), a few objects that begin with other sounds

Use the yellow yarn to make a large circle on the floor. Place all of the **Y** and non–**Y** objects inside the circle. Have the children name each object as you show it to the class. Repeat the word, emphasizing the beginning sound. As the objects are introduced to the class, place them on a table.

Each child comes up to the table, selects an object, and says its name. If it begins like yellow yarn, the child places it inside the yarn circle. If it does not begin like yellow yarn, he/she feeds it to the sound muncher. The child or the class makes the beginning sound of the non–**Y** object as it is being eaten.

Leave the yellow yarn and all of the **Y** objects out as a display in the classroom.

Introducing the Letter Y y *(cont.)*

Letter Centers

Yellow Pictures

Materials: paper, crayons, markers or paint

Children color or paint pictures of yellow things like the sun, bananas, pineapple, pears, apples, lemons, sunflowers, etc.

Yarn Designs

Materials: small pieces of cardboard, multicolored yarn, glue

Children glue yarn to the cardboard to form a pretty design.

Y y Play Dough

Materials: yellow play dough, yogurt lids, yardsticks

Children press yogurt lids and yardsticks into the play dough to form pictures and patterns. They can also roll the dough to form the capital and lowercase letters **Y y**.

was yummy!"

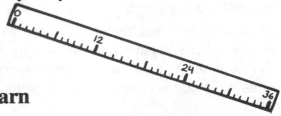

Let's Learn

Before they respond to each question or direction that you give them, ask the children to identify which word or words begin with a **Y**. Write the **Y** words on a wall chart or on the chalkboard.

Let's Talk

- Name a flavor of yogurt. (strawberry, cherry, blueberry, plain)
- Name something that is yellow. (a crayon, sun, lemon, pear)
- Name something that you could use yarn for. (knitting, leash, art project, hair bow)
- Name something that you think is yummy to eat.
- Name something that you think is yucky to eat.

Let's Move

- Move around the room like a yak.
- Nod your head to show yes.

Let's Pretend

Pretend to:
- mow and water the yard
- measure your classroom with a yardstick
- yawn

Let's Do

- Count yellow butterscotch candy pieces out to correspond with oral or written numbers.
- Take a survey on the children's favorite yellow fruit: banana, pear, apple or pineapple slice. Record the results on a "Yellow Fruit Graph."
- Make up a tongue twister using **y** words: *Yawning Yak yelled, "Yesterday's yogurt was yummy!"*

Introducing the Letter Y y *(cont.)*

Letter Y Picture Cards

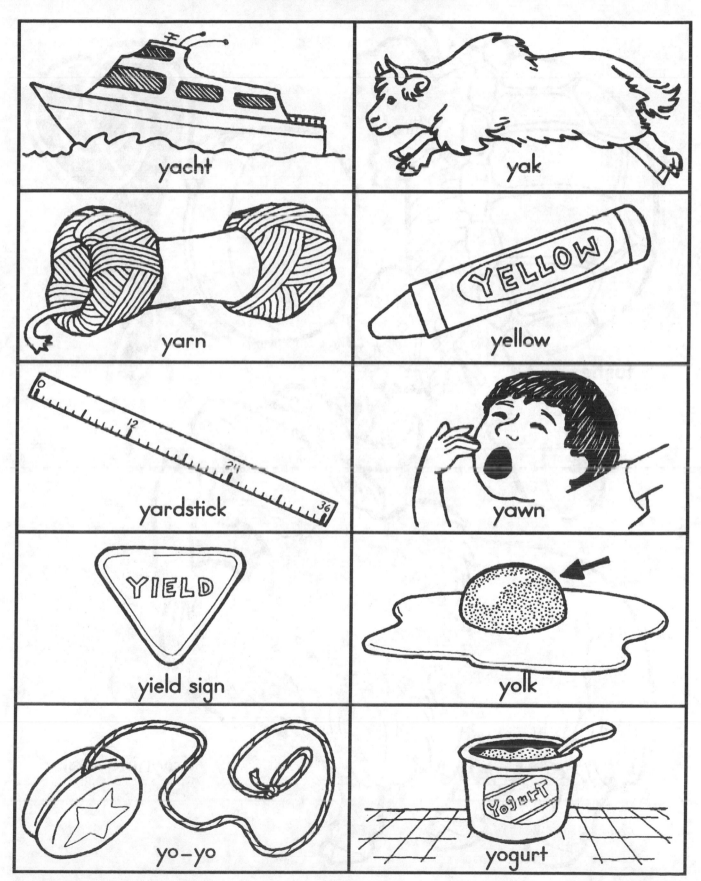

yacht

yak

yarn

yellow

yardstick

yawn

yield sign

yolk

yo-yo

yogurt

Introducing the Letter Y y (cont.)

Patterns

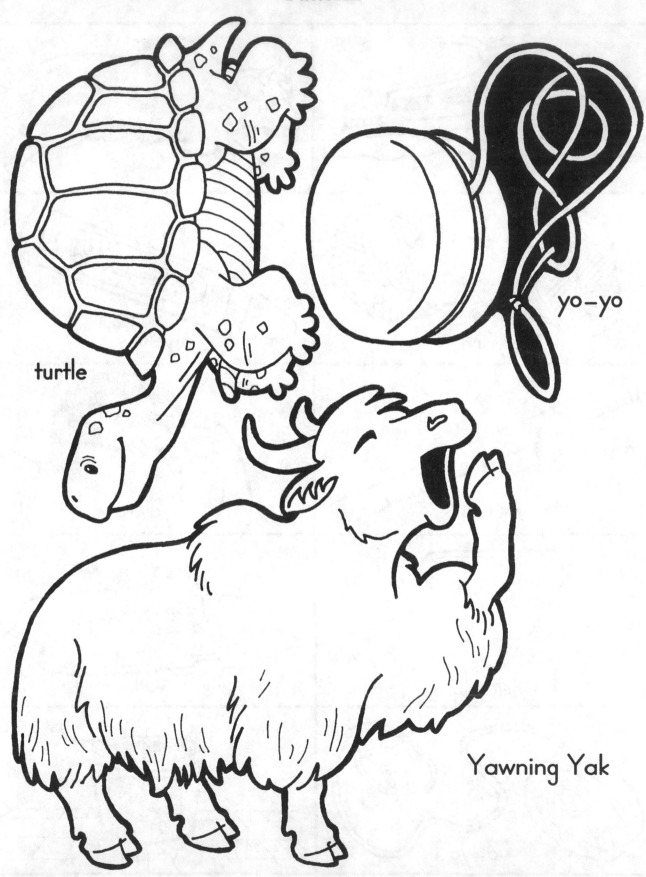

turtle

yo–yo

Yawning Yak

Introducing the Letter Z z

Letter Z Literature: *On Beyond Zebra!* by Dr. Seuss

Materials: paper, crayons, markers

After reading *On Beyond Zebra!* show the children the list of letters for people who don't stop at **Z** at the end of the book. Let them make up a name for the letter on the very last page. Have the children create their own letters, name them and draw what they means on their of papers.

What Do You Hear?

Materials: letter **Z** picture cards (reproduced, colored, and laminated)

Talk about the sound that the letter **Z** makes. Show the children each picture card and ask them to name each object. Repeat the word, emphasizing the **Z** sound.

Give each card to a child. Pick one child to come up in front of the class. That child will show the rest of the class the picture card he/she is holding. The class responds with the chant "What Do You Hear?"

Class: "Zipper, zipper, what do you hear?" (The student in front of the class looks at the remaining pictures and picks one to call next.)

Child: "I hear zero beginning like me."

Class: "Zero, zero, what do you hear?"

Child: "I hear zucchini beginning like me."

Continue until all of the picture cards have been called. The last child responds: "I hear the letter **Z** beginning with me."

The class adds: "We all hear the **Z** sound going z–z–z–z!"

Z Is a Zippy Letter!

Materials: big pieces of construction paper or poster board paper with a large capital and lowercase **Z** printed on each, glue, **Z** items (clear plastic zipper bag, zigzag fringe, real or foil zippers, addresses from mail with the zip codes highlighted, zoo animal crackers)

Divide the class into groups of four or five. Each group will glue **Z** items to the paper, covering the
Z z. When the glue dries, display them on a bulletin board or wall.

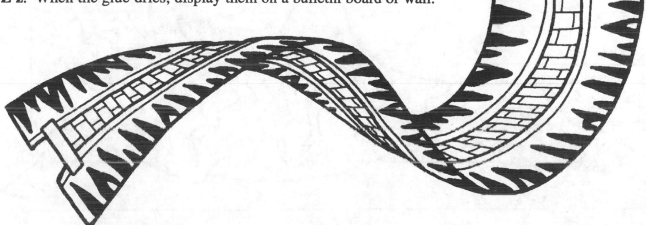

Introducing the Letter Z *(cont.)*

Bulletin Board

Materials: crayons or markers, paper, scissors, glue, magazines, copies of picture cards or other **Z** worksheets, one gallon-sized plastic "zipper" bag, sandwich-sized "zipper" bags for each child

Print the following directions: *Please fill a zipper bag with zesty pictures that begin with the letter **Z**.* Place the directions inside the gallon-sized zipper bag, seal it shut, and staple it to the center of the bulletin board.

Show the bulletin board to the children and explain the directions with them.

Have the children fill their bags with pictures that begin with the letter **z**, using pictures they have drawn, pictures cut from magazines, or worksheets they have colored. Staple their filled, sealed zipper bags onto the bulletin board.

Ask the children to search at home for additional **Z** pictures to add to the bulletin board.

Sounds and Pictures

Materials: Zippy Zebra (reproduced, colored, and laminated zebra pattern), large zigzag fringe, **Z** picture cards, some non–**Z** picture cards, Velcro, hole punch, picture board, sound muncher

Punch a hole at the top of each picture card and hot glue Velcro pieces onto the back of each picture card. Hot glue the matching Velcro pieces onto the zigzag fringe.

Place most of the **Z** picture cards and some non–**Z** picture cards on the picture board. Save a few to be added later.

Hang the zigzag fringe on the wall where the children can touch and look at it. Place the zebra by the fringe. Have the children gather by the zigzag, zebra, picture board, and sound muncher.

Tell the children: "I would like you to meet Zippy Zebra. Zippy Zebra is special because his stripes are zigzagged instead of straight like other zebras. His name is Zippy because when he runs, he zips past all of the other zebras, making a z–z–z–z sound. (Have the children make the z–z–z–z sound like Zippy makes as he runs.) He has brought in a piece of zigzag with him today because he needs our help. He wants his piece of zigzag to be filled with pictures that begin with the letter **Z**. Can you help him decorate his zigzag with pictures that start with the same sound as zebra, zigzag, and the sound he makes when he runs, z–z–z–z?"

Introducing the Letter Z z *(cont.)*

Sounds and Pictures *(cont.)*

Point to each picture on the picture board as the children tell you what is on each card. Repeat the word, emphasizing the beginning sound. Call the children one at a time to come up to the picture board and pick a card. If it begins with a **Z**, the child sticks it on the zigzag while Zippy Zebra and the children make his special z–z–z–z sound. If it does not begin with a **Z**, he/she feeds it to the sound muncher. The child or the class makes the beginning sound of the non–**Z** picture that is being eaten.

Leave Zippy Zebra and his zigzag out in the classroom. After you have done this activity several times, add some more **Z** pictures and several non–**Z** pictures to the zigzag.

Tell the children: "Zippy added some more pictures to his zigzag, but he is not sure if they all begin with the **Z** sound."

Point to each picture on the zigzag and have the class say the word with you. Ask the children to look at the zigzag and identify any pictures which need to be removed and fed to the sound muncher. Have the sound muncher and the children make the beginning sound of the non–**Z** picture as it is being eaten.

Sounds and Objects

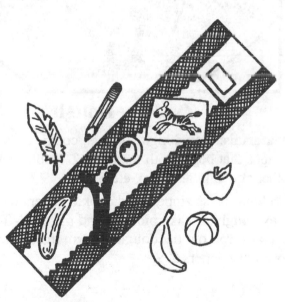

Materials: long piece of aluminum foil cut with pinking shears to resemble a zipper and laminated, objects that begin with the letter **Z** (zippers, zucchini, zipper baggies, paper zigzags and zeros, zip codes from letters), several objects that begin with other sounds

Place all of the **Z** objects and non–**Z** objects on the zipper. Have the children name each object as you show it to the class. Repeat the word, emphasizing the beginning sound. As the objects are introduced to the class, place them on a table.

The children come up to the table one at a time, pick out an object and say its name. If it begins like zipper, the child places it on the zipper. If it does not begin like zipper, he/she feeds it to the sound muncher. The child or the class makes the beginning sound of the non–**Z** object as it is being eaten.

Leave the zipper and all of the **Z** objects out as a display in the classroom.

Introducing the Letter Z *(cont.)*

Letter Centers

Z Is for Zero

Materials: paper with the capital and lowercase letters **Z z** printed on it, glue, any type of ringed cereal

Children glue "zeros" (ring-shaped cereal) down on top of the **Z z**, and let them dry.

Zoo

Materials: animal crackers, pre-slit foam meat trays, glue, yarn

Children glue animal crackers onto the foam meat trays, let them dry, slip yarn into slits, and wrap it from one end of the tray to the other to resemble bars on a zoo cage.

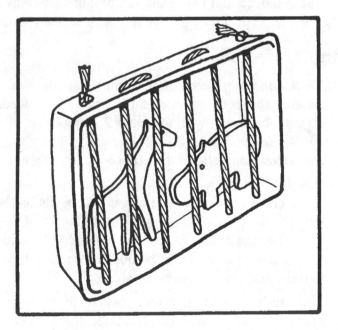

Zipper and Zigzag Rubbings

Materials: various lengths of zippers, zigzag fringe, paper and crayons

Children place paper on top of the zippers and zigzag fringe and then rub with crayons. Encourage the children to use different colors and to overlap.

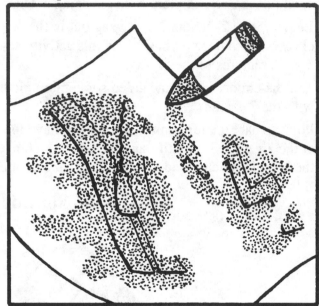

Z z Play Dough

Materials: play dough, zippers, cookie cutters in shapes that begin with the letter **Z** (zebras and other zoo animals, zero, etc.)

Children press zippers and cookie cutters into the play dough to make pictures and patterns. They can also roll out the dough to form the capital and lowercase letters **Z z**.

Let's Learn

Before they respond to each question or direction that you give them, ask the children to identify which word or words begin with a **Z**. Write the **Z** words on a wall chart or on the chalkboard.

Introducing the Letter Z *(cont.)*

Let's Learn *(cont.)*

Let's Talk

- If you could have a zillion of something, what would it be?
- Name something that has a zipper on it. (jeans, backpack, purse)
- Name something besides an animal that you might find in a zoo. (gift shop, concession stand, zoo keeper, cages)
- What is a zany thing that you or someone you know has done?

Let's Move

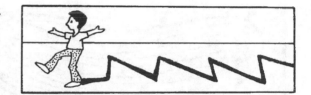

- Move around the room like a zebra, and a zebrafish.
- Zoom like a motorcycle around the room.
- Zip around the room like a race car driver.
- Walk around the room in a zigzag line.

Let's Pretend

Pretend to:

- zip up a sleeping bag and a book bag
- write your zip code on a letter and mail it
- plant zucchini in your garden

Let's Do

- Children count out zeros (ring-shaped cereal) to correspond with oral or written numbers.
- Make a list of animals that are in the zoo. Children pick their favorite animals and record their answers on a "Zoo Graph."
- Make up a tongue twister using **Z** words: *Zany Zebra's zoo zip code has zillions of zeros.*

	ZEBRA	KOALA	RHINO	WOLF	OKAPI	BISON	PANDA
JESSE			✔	✔			
KATE	✔	✔	✔	✔	✔	✔	✔
ROB			✔	✔	✔		
JOEL	✔		✔				
LEE		✔					✔
ANNIE	✔				✔		✔
MIKE			✔	✔			

Introducing the Letter Z *(cont.)*

Letter Z Picture Cards

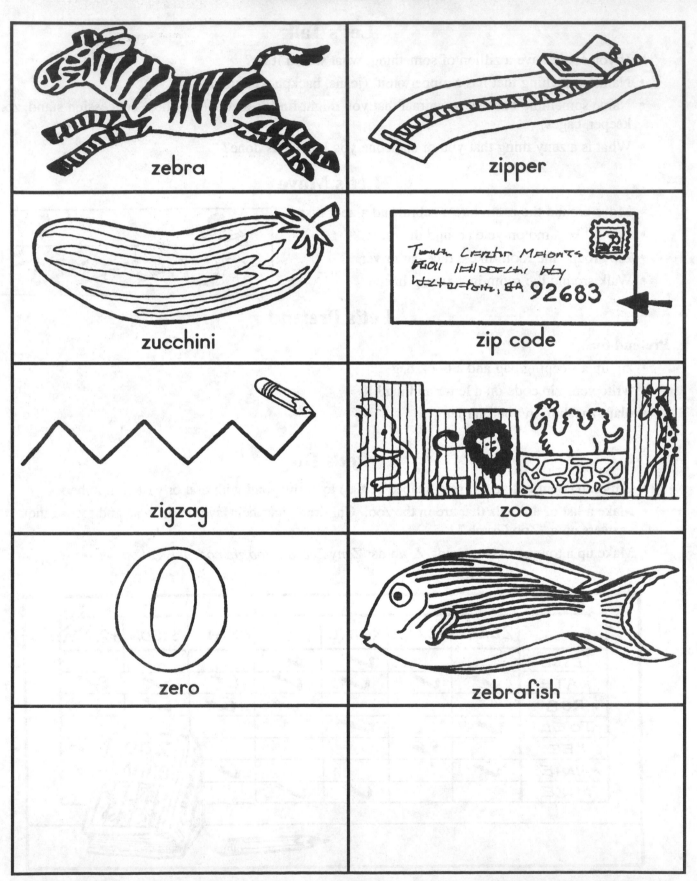

zebra

zipper

zucchini

zip code

zigzag

zoo

zero

zebrafish

Introducing the Letter Z *(cont.)*

Patterns

Zippy Zebra

Zero

Unit Management

Additional Vocabulary

Short A
albatross
antler
asparagus
atlas
ambulance
attic
avocado

B
backpack
bacon
badge
bag
ball
bamboo
banana
banjo
bank
barbed wire
barn
barrel
basket
basketball
bat
battery
beads
beans
beard
beaver
bed
beetle
bell
belt
bench
biscuit
board
boat
bologna
bolt
bone
bonnet
book
boomerang

boot
bottle
bow
bowl
box
boy
bubbles
bus
bush
buzzard

Hard C
cab
caboose
cage
cake
calendar
can
cane
canoe
cantaloupe
canteen
cap
card
cartoon
cassette
cauliflower
coal
cobweb
compass
cone
corn
couch
coyote
cup
curtains

Soft C
cedar
cellophane
cemetery
ceramics
cider
cinnamon
cylinder

cypress

D
daffodil
diaper
dime
dirt
doll
dollar
dolphin
dominoes
door
dot
dough
doughnut
dove

F
face
fawn
fern
ferret
flag
floor
flute
fly

Hard G
garlic
gift
grass

H
hammer
handle
harmonica
hat
hawk
heart
heel
helicopter
helmet
hill
hinge
hippopotamus
hog

hole
honey
hood
hoof
hook
horn
horse
horseshoe
hose
house
hummingbird
hyena

Short I
inch
Indian
invitation

Long I
ice skates
icing
iris
island
ivory

J
jack-o'-lantern
jaguar
janitor
jaw
jay
jellyfish
jet
jewelry
jug
jungle
junk

K
kale
kazoo
kernel
kid
kilt
kitchen
kiwi

Unit Management

Additional Vocabulary (cont.)

L
label
lace
lake
lamp
lasso
latch
lattice
lawnmower
leash
leather
lemonade
letter
lettuce
library
license plate
licorice
lightning
lime
line
linoleum
lint
lip
list
lobster
lock
locket
log
lollipop

M
maze
microwave
mink
mint
mongoose
monster
moss
moth
mustache

N
noodle
north

Short O
octagon
office
olive

Long O
oatmeal
oboe
ocean
odor
old
oleo
open
orangutan

P
paddle
pail
pajamas
palm
pamphlet
pancake
paper clip
paper
parakeet
pearl
peas
pebble
penny
pepper
perfume
pickles
pipe cleaner
plum
pocket
popcorn
postcard
potato chips
powder
pretzel
price tag
prunes
pudding
purse

R
rack
racket
raft
raisin
raspberry
recorder
rice
riffle
river
road
rock
ruffle

S
sack
saddle
salad
salamander
Santa
school
screw
seed
seesaw
seven
sink
six
skirt
sled
slide
slug
smoke
snail
snake
snow
spider
spinach
spoon
square
stamp
star
stick
stork
stove
swan

T
T-shirt
table
taco
tape
tarantula
telephone
ten
ticket
tie
toad
tooth
toys
train
trampoline
tree
triangle
trombone
trophy
truck
trumpet
tuba
two

Short U
uncle
up
uphill
upstairs

Long U
UPC symbol
utensil
Utah

V
vegetables
vaporizer
video
vinegar
vitamins
vowel
visor

W
wall

wallpaper
walnut
wasp
wheelchair
whisk
window
watermelon
wire
witch
wolf
woodpecker
world
worm
washcloth
water
wink

X
Xerxes
xylophone

Y
year
yeast
yarn
yard

Unit Management

Picture Card Pattern